THE TAX PLANNING ADVISORY SYSTEM

A proven 10-step framework for
accountants delivering strategic tax advice.

DARREN GLEESON

Copyright © 2025 Darren Gleeson
ISBN: 978-1-923078-92-5

Published by Vivid Publishing
A division of Fontaine Publishing Group
P.O. Box 948, Fremantle
Western Australia 6959
www.vividpublishing.com.au

NATIONAL
LIBRARY
OF AUSTRALIA

A catalogue record for this
book is available from the
National Library of Australia

This book is dedicated to the Father of AI
– John McCarthy

In 1956, John McCarthy, a visionary computer scientist, coined the term "**Artificial Intelligence**" at the famous Dartmouth Conference. His bold vision imagined a world where machines could simulate human intelligence, solving problems, learning from data, and supporting decision-making. Today, AI powers industries across the globe - from healthcare to finance, logistics to entertainment - and is rapidly transforming how we work and live.

McCarthy's legacy is not just about creating new technologies. It's about empowering people to make smarter decisions. His work laid the foundation for using AI to tackle complex challenges and improve outcomes in areas that matter most.

This same philosophy drives **TaxFitness** and the **Tax Planning Advisory System**. By combining decades of tax knowledge, over 300 proven tax strategies, and cutting-edge AI tools, TaxFitness helps accountants deliver strategic tax advice that was once only possible for top-tier firms.

AI is not here to replace accountants - it's here to **amplify** their expertise. It turns data into insights, recommendations into action, and complex tax strategies into clear, client-ready advice. Just as McCarthy envisioned, AI gives professionals a system to do more, think deeper, and deliver greater value.

As you read this book, remember that the power of AI lies not in the technology itself, but in **how you use it**. The Tax Planning Advisory System is your framework to harness this power - helping you become a true strategic advisor for your clients. Let McCarthy's legacy inspire you: use AI as a tool to drive innovation, improve outcomes, and create a lasting impact for the businesses you serve.

About TaxFitness

TaxFitness provides AI powered tax planning software. This is supported by marketing, resources and training courses.

Further details are available at www.taxfitness.com.au.

TaxFitness founders (left to right) – Darren Gleeson, Roydon Snelgar and Tracy James

Disclaimer

The contents are general information only. It is not intended to be taxation, accounting, business, financial, legal or other professional advice and should not be acted on or relied upon as such. Specific professional advice should be sought regarding particular circumstances and requirements, as the information may not be suitable or applicable to particular circumstances and should not be acted on or relied upon. The authors have used reasonable endeavours to ensure that the content is correct and current but do not guarantee that it is correct or current and will not be liable or responsible if it is not. In no event will the authors or any related entity of those persons, or any of their directors, principals, agents, employees or representatives, be liable for any loss, damage, costs or expense (whether direct or consequential) incurred as a result of or arising out of or in connection with this book and the content included in it in whole or in part including but not limited to any error, omission or misrepresentation. The authors also disclaim all representations and warranties, including but not limited to the quality, accuracy or completeness of the information of whatsoever nature and warranties of fitness for a particular purpose.

Table of Contents

20. Tax-saving investments

21. Tax-free retirement

1.

Introduction: Tax planning – from spreadsheets to strategy

'THE SECRET OF GETTING AHEAD IS GETTING STARTED'
– MARK TWAIN (AMERICAN AUTHOR, 1835 – 1910).

1. How can I save tax?

Ever had a client ask, "How can I save tax? "-and you didn't have a clear answer? That moment stays with you.

For years, tax planning has been a challenge for accountants-manual spreadsheets, broken formulas, hours lost chasing numbers, and that sinking feeling you might have missed something. I know the feeling.

Back in 2017, I realised tax planning needed more than just tools. It needed a framework-a step-by-step process that any accountant could follow to deliver strategic, proactive advice. Not just compliance work-real value that helps clients save tax, build wealth, and grow their businesses.

That's how the Tax Planning 10-Step Framework was born.

This framework isn't theory. It's practical. It's been tested in accounting firms across Australia, helping them:

- Identify tax-saving opportunities with confidence.
- Apply the right strategies for each client-without the guesswork.
- Present advice clearly, so clients understand it-and take action.

- Build stronger client relationships and generate $30k to $100k+ in new advisory fees every year.

The 10-Step Framework will guide you through:
- How to structure tax planning engagements the right way.
- The questions to ask, the data to collect, and how to analyse it.
- How to select from over 300 tax strategies-and match them to each client.
- How to model tax savings, show the impact, and present it in a way that sells.

This book will walk you through the framework-step by step-so you can deliver tax planning with confidence.

Yes, tools like TaxFitness exist to make the process faster-but this book isn't about software. It's about giving you the system-a clear, repeatable process that turns tax planning from an afteli-hought into a high-value service.

Let's dive in. I'll show you exactly how it works.

Darren Gleeson
CEO, TaxFitness

2.
What is tax planning?

'I AM THE WISEST MAN ALIVE, FOR I KNOW ONE THING,
AND THAT IS THAT I KNOW NOTHING'
– PLATO (GREEK PHILOSOPHER, 427 BC – 347 BC).

1. Definition

ATO definition:

Tax planning or tax-effective investing is the arrangement of financial affairs to keep taxes to a minimum. Tax planning is legitimate when done within the letter and spirit of the law.

Chat GPT definition:

Tax planning is the proactive and strategic structuring of an individual's or business's financial affairs to legally minimise tax liability, optimise after-tax outcomes, and improve financial efficiency and wealth creation.

Taxfitness definition (what's included)

1. Wealth creation (business and/or investments).
2. Saving future tax (before retirement).
3. Saving future tax (after retirement).
4. CGT on business and personal assets.
5. Ensuring tax compliance.
6. Resolving tax-related issues, i.e. Div 7a loans.
7. Forecasting tax liabilities.

8. Ensuring cash flow is available for a tax payment schedule.
9. Wealth and asset structures.
10. Saving stamp duty, payroll tax, and land tax.
11. Saving tax – prior to 30th June.

2. Tax planning versus tax compliance

Tax planning is different from tax compliance.

Tax compliance involves meeting legal requirements regarding taxes and reporting. Lodging a tax return is a common example of tax compliance.

On the other hand, **tax planning** involves assessing your clients' unique circumstances against over 300 tax strategies and selecting the ones that can be implemented to achieve savings and benefits. Tax planning strategies use various legal deductions, exemptions, structures, and tax-effective investing. Each strategy has an implementation process to follow, and only accounting professionals genuinely skilled at tax planning know how these work.

3. Do all accountants and tax agents provide tax planning?

No, only those who specialise in the level of knowledge required can provide tax planning properly. It is the same as a GP doctor versus a specialist. Similar to a medical specialist, a tax planning specialist has very specific skills.

As a public practice accountant, having these skills provides a competitive edge in the industry.

4. What are the benefits of tax planning?

Valuable tax savings are achieved with tax planning – These legal tax saving strategies can save your client tax if correctly implemented. This significantly reduces the tax the client needs to pay and creates a position for ongoing tax planning services to the client. It becomes a regular service to the client and increases fees for your practice.

Tax planning assists your clients in meeting their Australian Taxation Office (ATO) obligations to avoid penalties and fines – Examples include:
- Business registration
- GST
- Income tax
- PAYG withholding
- Superannuation
- Fringe benefits tax (FBT)
- Record keeping
- Fuel tax credits
- State and territory taxes – payroll tax and land tax
- Other reporting – taxable payments reporting

Tax planning reviews and audits your clients' business structures – Their unique circumstances are assessed to determine the optimum business structures to save tax and protect their assets.

During the tax planning process client 'wants/aspirations' are identified. The client 'wants' enable you to determine what's important to the clients and tailor services to satisfy their wants.
Client wants may include:
- Minimise tax now and in the future.
- Increase profit. How much?
- Grow sales.
- Protect assets from creditors, lawsuits or divorce.
- Increase cash flow.
- Work less, less stress, lifestyle.
- Increase wealth. How much?

- Security and peace of mind.
- Estate planning – looking after loved ones.
- Succession planning, or selling the business.
- Being able to work in the business as an owner instead of in it.
- Achieve personal goals. What are they?
- Finance to purchase house, investments or refinance at lower interest rate.

5. How the tax planning service works (how to explain it to clients)

Process:

1. Complete the Interview Checklist to understand their correct financial position and client 'wants' (what they want to achieve and where they want to get to).
2. Review their accounting software file or other documents.
3. For business owners, determine an accurate year-to-date profit for the business and extrapolate the year-to-date profit for the financial year.
4. Estimate the current year's income of all the individuals and entities that comprise the overall structure. Typically, this includes the client, their spouse, children, partnerships, companies, trusts, and SMSF.
5. Apply a combination of tax planning knowledge and specialised software to select appropriate tax planning strategies to reduce tax.
6. Determine the optimum mix of gross salary and superannuation contributions for the current year.
7. Conduct a compliance audit to ensure ATO obligations are met.
8. Where there are business structures review and audit these.
9. Produce a tax planning report. The report quantifies the

exact tax savings from implementing the selected tax strategies and details the processes involved in implementing these to achieve the results.

10. Meet with the client to discuss the report and determine the strategies they would like to implement. Assist with strategy implementation where appropriate.

11. Provide early identification of business compliance, risk factors (if any), legal position and performance factors.

6. Tax planning 'v' tax avoidance

When it comes to helping clients minimise tax, the difference between tax planning and tax avoidance isn't just technical—it's about ethics, intent, and risk.

Tax planning: smart, strategic, and compliant

Tax planning is the legal and ethical process of organising your clients' financial affairs to legitimately reduce their tax liability. It's proactive, strategic, and aligns with the intent of the law.

It involves:

- Choosing the right business structure
- Timing income and expenses effectively
- Accessing available deductions, offsets, and concessions
- Planning for superannuation contributions and asset ownership

In other words, it's the kind of work that adds real value to your clients and positions you as a trusted adviser.

Tax avoidance: technically legal, ethically questionable

Tax avoidance, on the other hand, involves using the tax system to reduce tax in ways that may be within the letter of the law – but go against its spirit. It often relies on complex schemes, loopholes, or aggressive structuring that push right up to the edge of legality. It's not tax evasion (which is outright illegal), but it's risky. The ATO can apply anti-avoidance provisions if it believes the main purpose of an arrangement is to avoid tax.

What do people think about tax avoidance?

Community attitudes toward tax avoidance are mixed – and shifting:

- Some see it as smart financial management.
- Others see it as unethical behaviour that shifts the tax burden unfairly.
- Public reaction often depends on how aggressive or artificial the scheme appears, and whether the taxpayer is seen as "doing their fair share."

In high-profile cases (especially involving large corporations), tax avoidance can trigger public backlash, reputational damage, and even lead to law reform. For advisers: this is where you make a real difference. Clients don't just want to pay less tax – they want to do it the right way.

Your role is to:

- Educate them on the difference between tax planning and tax avoidance
- Build strategies that are effective and defensible.

- Stay up to date with ATO rulings and legislative intent
- Avoid the short-term wins that come with long-term risks

The bottom line

If your strategies work because of the law, that's tax planning. If they only work because of a loophole, that's tax avoidance – and the ATO is watching. Make sure your clients understand the distinction and always choose the ethical, sustainable path.

7. Size of the Australian accounting market - $27.1b

The IBIS Australia 'Accounting Services in Australia' report for the 2024 financial year shows the following industry dynamics:

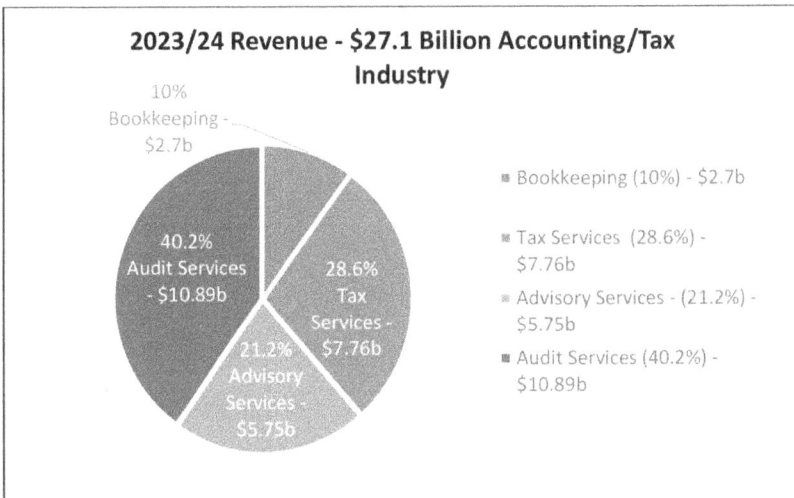

2023/24 Revenue - $27.1 Billion Accounting/Tax Industry

10% Bookkeeping - $2.7b

40.2% Audit Services - $10.89b

28.6% Tax Services - $7.76b

21.2% Advisory Services - $5.75b

- Bookkeeping (10%) - $2.7b
- Tax Services (28.6%) - $7.76b
- Advisory Services - (21.2%) - $5.75b
- Audit Services (40.2%) - $10.89b

Key factors:

- Revenue - $27.1b
- Industry revenue for the four key service lines:
  - o Audit services (40.2%) - $10.89b
  - o Tax services (28.6%) - $7.76b
  - o Advisory services (21.2%) - $5.75b
  - o Bookkeeping services (10%) - $2.7b

- Businesses – 36,903
- Employees – 159,000 ($10.3b wages)

The Big Four accounting practices (PWC Australia, EY, Deloitte, and KPMG) generate 40% of their revenue from advisory services (tax planning and business advisory). Australia's next 100 largest practices generate 20% of their revenue from advisory services.

8. Size of the Australian tax planning market - $600m

For the year ended 30th June 2024, 45,333 tax agents (RTA) and 17,000 tax (financial) advisers generated $600 million in tax planning revenue. Tax planning accounted for 7.7% of the year's $7.76 billion tax services revenue.

As only 20% of accounting practices generate any tax planning revenue, the potential size of the Australian tax planning market is $1 - $1.5 billion.

This bar graph shows the break-up of the $7.76b of Tax Services (shown in green on the pie graph)

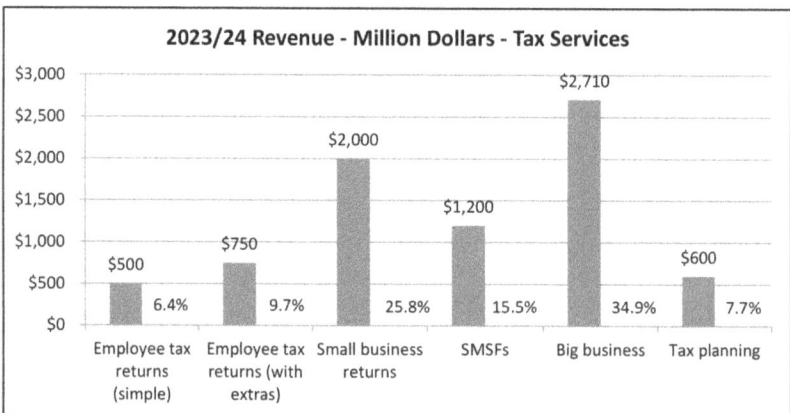

2023/24 Revenue - Million Dollars - Tax Services

Category	Revenue	Percentage
Employee tax returns (simple)	$500	6.4%
Employee tax returns (with extras)	$750	9.7%
Small business returns	$2,000	25.8%
SMSFs	$1,200	15.5%
Big business	$2,710	34.9%
Tax planning	$600	7.7%

9. Tax planning software

Over the last twenty years, every task, function, and service in the average accounting practice has changed dramatically. The personal computer and associated software have brought enormous efficiencies in preparing financial statements, budgeting, and tax returns. Today, no accountants perform these tasks manually.

Tax planning has also greatly benefited from computerisation. Tax planning software has now improved an ad hoc, manual, time-consuming process to a new level of efficiency and effectiveness. Tax planning software aims to simplify tax-related tasks, optimise tax positions, and ensure compliance with tax laws and regulations. It streamlines the tax planning process, saves time, reduces errors, and helps users make informed financial decisions to minimise tax liabilities and maximise tax savings.

Tax planning software typically offers:

- **Tax calculation and projection:** Tax planning software can calculate and project tax liabilities based on user-provided financial data. It considers various tax rules, rates, and thresholds to estimate the amount of tax owed or refunded, allowing users to plan their finances accordingly.
- **Integration with accounting systems:** This enables the financial data to be seamlessly imported (this eliminates manual data entry and ensures accuracy and consistency).
- **Tax strategy selection/optimisation:** The software identifies and suggests available deductions, exemptions, and offsets to help users maximise their tax savings.
- **Scenario analysis:** Users can simulate different financial scenarios within the software to evaluate their tax implications. This allows for strategic decision-making by assessing the potential impact of various financial choices on their tax positions, such as investments, retirement contributions, or business decisions.

- **Reporting:** The software generates reports that detail the tax savings generated from implementing the selected tax strategies, as well as the step-by-step process to legally and effectively implement each strategy.
- **Tax law compliance:** Tax planning software keeps track of tax laws and regulations, ensuring compliance with the latest requirements. It incorporates changes in tax legislation to accurately reflect the current tax environment and help users meet their obligations.
- **Data organisation and storage:** Tax planning software provides a centralised platform for organising and storing tax-related information.

3.

Why create a tax planning division?

'IT DOES NOT MATTER HOW SLOWLY YOU GO
AS LONG AS YOU DO NOT STOP'
– CONFUCIUS (CHINESE PHILOSOPHER, 551 BC – 479 BC).

1. Generate an extra $30,000 - $100,000 in fees first year

A good first-year target is $30,000 - $100,000 in tax planning revenue when establishing a new tax planning division. As a new practice service, any fees you generate from tax planning will increase your existing fee base (and goodwill value).

The opportunities to generate tax planning fees exist in your current client base - you don't need more new clients at this stage. Instead, you just need to find out the client 'wants' and then help them achieve them (which will require the provision of various tax planning and business advisory services).

2. Tax planning and business advisory services could increase your existing fees by 100%

In suburban accounting practices across Australia, a startling trend has emerged: around 80% of firms are generating minimal revenue from tax planning and business advisory services.

Despite having loyal client bases and years of experience, these practices remain heavily focused on compliance work-BAS, tax returns, and financial statements-leaving significant revenue, profit, and business value untapped. But here's the opportunity - shifting to an advisory-first model could double a practice's total fees.

The compliance trap

Most suburban firms operate in a cycle of deadlines-completing tax returns, meeting lodgement dates, and keeping up with the ATO's demands. While this work is essential, it's also commoditised. Clients shop around on price, not value. Profit margins are often thin, and firm owners find themselves working harder every year for the same or sometimes less reward. Worse, this compliance-heavy model limits growth. There's a ceiling on how many tax returns one team can prepare. And when growth relies purely on volume, burnout is inevitable.

Why advisory is the game-changer

Advisory services, especially tax planning and business advisory-are the key to breaking out of the compliance grind. When done right, these services deliver immense value to clients. A simple tax planning strategy can save a business thousands, and good advice on structure, cash flow, or growth can be transformative. Clients are willing to pay for advice that improves their bottom line and they're more likely to stay loyal to the accountant who provides it.

Here's the kicker: firms that aim to have 50% of their revenue come from advisory services often see their total fees increase by 100%.

This is because:

- Advisory work commands higher fees and margins.
- It builds deeper client relationships, leading to more referrals.
- It creates recurring revenue streams, especially when packaged as monthly or annual subscriptions.

- It increases goodwill value, as buyers place a premium on firms with advisory income.

The 50/50 revenue model

Adopting a 50/50 revenue model-where 50% comes from compliance and 50% from advisory-is both achievable and transformative.

Let's break it down:

- If your current practice earns $400,000 in revenue, and 90% of that is compliance, you may only be generating $40,000 from advisory.
- Moving to a 50/50 model would lift advisory revenue to $360,000-a nine-fold increase-and potentially increase total revenue to $700,000 or more.
- That extra $300,000 in high-margin revenue significantly improves profitability, cash flow, and business valuation.

Getting started

The transition doesn't happen overnight, but it starts with a mindset shift. Stop seeing yourself purely as a compliance provider, and start positioning your firm as a trusted advisor.

Here's how to start:

1. Introduce simple tax planning services before 30 June.
2. Offer quarterly business reviews to existing business clients.
3. Package services into fixed-fee monthly subscriptions.
4. Train your team to identify and recommend strategies proactively.
5. Use tools and technology that strean1line advisory delivery.

Final thoughts

If you're in the 80% of suburban practices with minimal advisory revenue, now is the time to change. Advisory is not just a buzzword-it's the future of the profession. It's how you grow fees, increase profits, and build a practice that's both valuable and sustainable.

Want help getting there? TaxFitness gives you the strategies, systems, and support to make advisory services the most profitable part of your firm.

3. 80% of taxpayers can legally reduce the amount of tax they pay

Business owners can typically reduce the amount of tax they pay. Whether they do so, or not is due to three factors:

- Their desire to save tax - how important is it to them?
- Will they make the necessary changes to save tax? For example, will they change their business structures or refinance their loans?
- Do they have the funds available to implement the tax-saving strategies? For example, are funds available to contribute to superannuation?

4. Increases client retention and generates new clients from word-of-mouth referrals

Most services accountants provide are compulsory form-filling that adds little to no value. Not surprisingly, clients don't appreciate or highly value these services.

In contrast, value-added services, such as tax planning and business advisory, are highly valued by clients. (Once the accountant has demonstrated how these services help the client achieve their wants/objectives.) Why? Because they meet one test – they add value to the client.

To pass the value-added test, the service or product must generate value for the client at least three times (3X) the cost. Ideally 5 to 10 times.

5. No extra licensing or registrations are required

Registered tax agents with the Tax Practitioners Board can provide tax planning services with <u>no extra licences</u> required.

In contrast, practices expanding their services to include SMSF auditing, financial planning or finance broking are all subject to additional licensing or registrations. This imposes annual costs of $5,000 - $48,000 pa for licencing, training, software, support and admin services.

6. Your current compliance tax knowledge is the base level foundation upon which tax planning expertise can be readily built

Registered tax agents should have good base-level knowledge covering income, deductions, exemptions, and structures. Of course, each accountant's overall knowledge level will vary greatly. This is supported by the ATO's 'Individuals not in Business Tax Gap Report,' which found that 78% of tax agent-prepared returns have errors.

To your base-level knowledge of tax planning, you need to add the expertise to:
- Understand 300+ tax strategies (what they are, how they work and what clients they are suitable for).
- Problem-solve and work through the options to add value to the client's circumstances.
- Educate your clients on tax planning in general and the tax savings they can achieve.
- Communicate/sell the achievable benefits to the client.

7. Opportunity to differentiate yourself from your competitors

Three things need to occur for a differentiation strategy to be considered successful.

- **Firstly**, it must move your service from competing based primarily on price to competing on non-price factors such as service quality, service levels, brand name, service innovation, service features, or distribution channels.

  (Service innovation involves offering new services that clients need but are not currently provided by your competitors. Tax planning fits this to a 'T'.)

- **Secondly**, customers and potential customers must have their needs wholly met by that service to such a degree that competitors are rendered completely ineffective.

- **Thirdly**, the firm snowballs by easily acquiring new clients, and the financial numbers confirm this.

4.

Tax planning process

'GENIUS IS ONE PERCENT INSPIRATION,
AND NINETY-NINE PERCENT PERSPIRATION'

– THOMAS A. EDISON (AMERICAN INVENTOR, 1847 – 1931)

1. Flow chart of the 10-step tax planning process

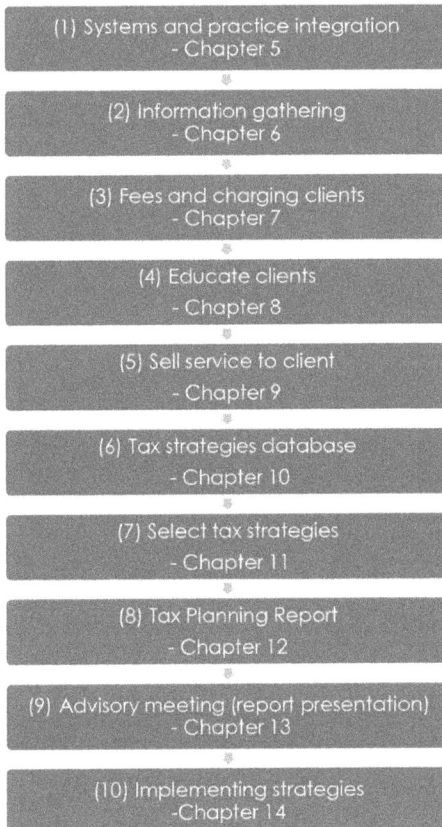

(1) Systems and practice integration
- Chapter 5

(2) Information gathering
- Chapter 6

(3) Fees and charging clients
- Chapter 7

(4) Educate clients
- Chapter 8

(5) Sell service to client
- Chapter 9

(6) Tax strategies database
- Chapter 10

(7) Select tax strategies
- Chapter 11

(8) Tax Planning Report
- Chapter 12

(9) Advisory meeting (report presentation)
- Chapter 13

(10) Implementing strategies
-Chapter 14

Step 1 - Systems and practice integration

'THE BEGINNING IS THE MOST IMPORTANT PART OF THE WORK'

– PLATO

You are at STEP 1

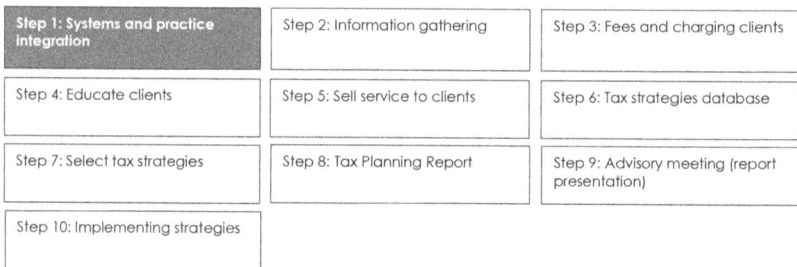

Step 1: Systems and practice integration	Step 2: Information gathering	Step 3: Fees and charging clients
Step 4: Educate clients	Step 5: Sell service to clients	Step 6: Tax strategies database
Step 7: Select tax strategies	Step 8: Tax Planning Report	Step 9: Advisory meeting (report presentation)
Step 10: Implementing strategies		

1. The objective of systems

Step 1 of the tax planning process is 'systems and practice integration'. Like all practice services, tax planning must be systemised to be efficient and effective. Failure to do this results in:

- Ad hoc service with no quality control.
- Few tax plans.
- Services are only provided to a few clients instead of offered to everyone.
- Low fees (even no fees in many cases)are charged due to a lack of confidence and low value provided to clients.
- Inefficiencies and too much time spent on the fees generated.

- Inability to highlight the value and your expertise, so low client satisfaction.
- TASA breaches due to inadequate documentation of advice.

Systemisation is not a new or foreign concept to accounting practices. Most practices have systemised how they prepare tax returns, financials, BASs, etc. Experience has taught us that a lack of systems results in inefficiencies, wasted time, unhappy clients, lower revenue, and lower profits.

As Ray Kroc, the founder of McDonald's, said, 'Just follow the system'.

Research shows accounting practices providing adhoc tax planning and business advisory services (i.e. without systems) are on average 70% as profitable as compliance-only practices.

In contrast, practices providing systemised tax planning and business advisory services are 200% more profitable than compliance-only practices.

Practice Profitability %

	Compliance + adhoc tax planning and/or business advisory	Compliance-only practice	Compliance + systemised tax planning & business advisory
Profitability %	70	100	300
Average Partner profit	$238,000 pa	$340,000 pa	$1,020,000 pa

2. The objective of practice integration

Overview	The tax planning process starts with systems and practice integration. Failure to effectively integrate tax planning services into the practice results in: • Tax planning being seasonal, only done in May/June of each financial year. Trying to provide the service in such a short timeframe results in capacity issues/bottlenecks and forgoes tax planning fees. • Only offering and providing the service to a few select clients. This limits tax planning revenue. • Minimal tax planning revenue (for the reasons explained in this section). • Limited learning and development - it's hard to develop a skill if it is practised so infrequently. The 5 steps to integrate tax planning into your practice are described below.
Step 1	Embed the service into compliance delivery (which is done by following the systems detailed in this manual).
Step 2	Ensure tax planning is done 12 months of the year (just like all other proactive services). Workflow is more even, efficiency/processing steady and revenue is maximised.
Step 3	Offer the service to all clients, don't prejudge which clients will be interested.
Step 4	Commit to making tax planning a substantial revenue generator for the practice. 20% of practice revenue is achievable.
Step 5	Allocate the time to develop your skills and expertise.

3. Interview checklists

A key reason practices fail when trying to sell tax planning and business advisory services to their clients is they don't understand their clients. They lack insight into both the client's current financial position and what they want to achieve. Consequently, they try and sell clients services that they neither need nor want (but are surprised by the poor results).

To be successful in providing tax planning and business advisory services, a practice needs to rectify this deficiency. Thankfully it's as simple as collecting the information in the interview checklist.

For the first year this will take approximately 10 minutes per client. In subsequent years the form will just need updating which should only take 5 minutes per client.

Completing the interview checklist enables us to understand our clients:

- Current financial position.
- Their 'wants' (what is important to them and what they would like to achieve).

The interview checklist should be completed for every client.

4. Three compliance quality control checklists

In **Section 5.2** we discussed the benefits of fully integrating tax planning services into your practice. An easy first step is to include the three quality control checklists in your compliance delivery process.

The three quality control checklists are:

- Business quality control checklist.
- BAS quality control checklist.
- Individual quality control checklist.

We recommend that the quality control checklists are provided to all clients when their compliance service is complete. This can be at the meeting for discussion and signing, or when the documents are emailed to clients for signing. The benefits of this are two-fold.

- Reinforces to the client the process and work undertaken to provide the compliance services (tax return, financial statements, BAS). Clients generally have no idea what accountants actually do for them as they only see the final process or outcome, i.e. tax return).
- Puts the client 'wants' questions in front of the client (up to five times per year for business clients). This non-intrusive repetition gets the client thinking about what's important to them.

5. Australian tax planning tools

2017	2015	2014	2013
TaxFitness	Change GPS	Business Fitness How Now	Tax Strategist

2013	2012	2011	1985
QuickBooks (AU)	MYOB Practice	Xero Tax + XPM	Microsoft Excel

Summary of tax planning tools:
- Microsoft Excel – dominates for custom, DIY solutions, but is labour-intensive.
- Xero, MYOB, QuickBooks and Business Fitness – basic planning via custom templates.
- Tax Strategist & Change GPS – good products.
- TaxFitness – AI, automation, benchmarking, marketing, resources and training.

6. Comparision of Excel 'v' TaxFitness for tax planning

Feature/Factor	Excel	TaxFitness Software
Customisation	Full control over design and formulas	Structured templates (with some customization)
Cost	One-off purchase or free (Google Sheets)	Ongoing subscription (annual or monthly)
Offline Access	Yes	Internet access usually required
Speed for One Client	Fast if simple; slow if complex	Extremely fast (prebuilt strategies + automation)
Handling Many Clients	Cumbersome; manual tracking	Efficient dashboard and client management
Professionalism of Reports	Depends on user skill	Always polished, branded, and consistent
Audit Trail / Compliance	Manual setup needed	Built-in documentation and referencing
Updating for Tax Law Changes	Manual, error-prone updates required	Automatic updates (e.g., tax rates, thresholds)
Benchmarking and Advisory Tools	Not built-in	Integrated into system
Scalability Across a Firm	Difficult (version control issues)	Easy (multi-user access, team workflows)

6.

Step 2 – Information gathering

*'WITHOUT KNOWLEDGE ACTION IS USELESS A
ND KNOWLEDGE WITHOUT ACTION IS FUTILE'*

– ABU BAKR (LEADER, 573 – 634)

You are at STEP 2

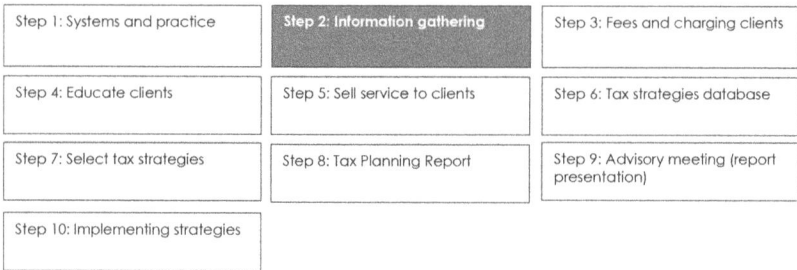

Step 1: Systems and practice	Step 2: Information gathering	Step 3: Fees and charging clients
Step 4: Educate clients	Step 5: Sell service to clients	Step 6: Tax strategies database
Step 7: Select tax strategies	Step 8: Tax Planning Report	Step 9: Advisory meeting (report presentation)
Step 10: Implementing strategies		

1. Understanding the client's current financial position

Step 2 of the tax planning process is 'information gathering'. A key reason practices fail when trying to sell tax planning and business advisory services to their clients is they don't understand their clients. They lack insight into both the client's current financial position and what they want to achieve. Consequently, they try and sell clients services they neither need nor want (it is therefore no surprise that the client rejects these services).

To be successful in providing tax planning and business advisory services, a practice needs to rectify this deficiency. Collecting information in the interview checklist solves this problem.

The interview checklist collects the following information on the client's current financial position:

Client	Spouse	Entity 1 (if applicable compile for each entity)
➤ Goals (short-term and long-term). ➤ Children, parents and dependents. ➤ Assets (includes business value). ➤ Liabilities ➤ Income ➤ Expenses	➤ Goals (short-term and long-term) ➤ Children, parents and dependents. ➤ Assets (includes business value). ➤ Liabilities ➤ Income ➤ Expenses	➤ Goals (short-term and long-term) ➤ Directors, trustees, shareholders and beneficiaries ➤ Assets ➤ Liabilities ➤ Income ➤ Expenses

2. Understanding what is important to the client

The client 'wants/aspirations' enable us to find out what is important to a specific client. Everyone is different, so until we have this information, we know nothing and cannot help the client.

We use the interview checklist to collect the information on the 13 client 'wants.

- Minimise tax now and in the future.
- Increase profit. How much?
- Grow sales.
- Protect assets from creditors, lawsuits or divorce.
- Increase cash flow.
- Work less, less stress, lifestyle.
- Increase wealth. How much?
- Security and peace of mind.
- Estate planning – looking after loved ones.
- Succession planning, or selling the business.
- Being able to work in the business as an owner instead of in it.
- Achieve personal goals. What are they?

- Finance to purchase house, investments or refinance at lower interest rates.

3. Interview checklist

Completing the interview checklist enables us to understand our clients:

- Current financial position
- Their 'wants' (what is important to them and what they would like to achieve).

The interview checklist should be completed for:

- All business clients (i.e. 100%).
- Individual high income earners, rental property owners and the asset rich.

Ideally the interview checklist will be completed by the accountant when seeing the client for a compliance tax meeting. Alternatively, the checklist can be emailed to the client to complete and return.

For the first year the interview checklist will take 10-15 minutes per client to complete. In subsequent years the form just needs updating, which is a 5 minute job.

4. Essential client information

1.	**Members**—All the individuals and entities make up the client's overall structure. Typically, this includes the client, their spouse, children, partnerships, companies, trusts, and SMSFs.
2.	**The 2021-2025 historical financial data for all the members (if available).** Ideally, this information will be imported from their Xero, MYOB or Quickbooks accounting software file (the quickest and easiest method) for business owners. Alternatively, this can be done manually.
Notes	Consequently, preparing tax planning and business advisory reports for these clients in subsequent years will be super quick (80% time saving for second and subsequent years).

Information needed annually:

1.	For business owners, determine an accurate year-to-date profit for the business and extrapolate it to the financial year.
2.	Estimate the current year's income of all the individuals and entities that comprise the overall structure.
3.	Estimate the members' current year tax paid (PAYG withholding and PAYG instalments).
4.	Update/revise the members' current year assets and liabilities (personal and business). Approximate figures are okay.

5. Reasons why we gather the client information

- We need to find out the client's current financial situation and their client 'wants' (what they want to achieve), and then we can help them work out how to achieve their goals.
- Listing all the individuals and entities that comprise the

client's structure enables us to provide tax planning to the whole group. It gives us a complete picture of the client, their spouse, children, partnerships, companies, trusts, and SMSFs.

- Knowing the client's estimated current-year taxable income provides us with their estimated annual tax expense. From this starting point, we aim to reduce their tax expense through effective tax planning.

- Knowing the client's assets and liabilities (and the individuals and entities that own them) highlights tax planning opportunities. For example, transferring a spouse's private motor vehicle to a business entity will create ongoing tax savings of $2,500 - $3,000 pa. In addition, for vehicles valued at less than $20,000, this creates a one-off deduction equal to the vehicle's value.

- Finding out the client's expected future tax profile is useful. This information gives us insight into whether we should focus on tax strategies that provide a one-off or ongoing tax deduction. We could have two clients with the same taxable income this year who want to reduce their taxable income by the same amount. If one is 65 and retiring this year, his or her future tax profile will be different from that of a 35-year-old business owner who has another 30 years of paying taxes ahead of him or her.

- Knowing the client's funds for implementing tax strategies is useful as money enhances the client's tax planning options. Although some tax strategies don't require cash outflow, 50% do. For example, salary sacrificing pre-tax wages into super is a highly popular and effective tax planning strategy. But if the client requires all their wage income to live on and has no investment funds available, this tax strategy (no matter how attractive and effective) is not an option.

6. How to gather the client information

This can be done by:

1.	Complete the interview checklist when seeing the client for a compliance tax meeting. Alternatively, the checklist can be emailed to the client to complete and return.
2.	Review the client's tax returns and financial statements you have on hand and extract the relevant information. Ninety per cent of the required information will already be on hand.
3.	Ask the client for any extra information you require when you see them to prepare or discuss their compliance tax returns. Alternatively, please pick up the phone and call them. This will typically be required to get details on all the group members' private assets and liabilities and their respective market values.
4.	Email the client requesting the extra information you require.

7.

Step 3 - Fees and charging clients

'MONEY IS NOT THE MOST IMPORTANT THING IN LIFE,
BUT IT'S REASONABLY CLOSE TO OXYGEN ON THE
'GOTTA HAVE IT' SCALE'
– ZIG ZIGLAR (AMERICAN AUTHOR, 1926 – 2012).

You are at STEP 3

Step 1: Systems and practice	Step 2: Information gathering	**Step 3: Fees and charging clients**
Step 4: Educate clients	Step 5: Sell service to clients	Step 6: Tax strategies database
Step 7: Select tax strategies	Step 8: Tax Planning Report	Step 9: Advisory meeting (report presentation)
Step 10: Implementing strategies		

1. The objective of fees and charging clients

Step 3 of the tax planning process is 'fees and charging clients'. This chapter is all about how we calculate the fee and charge clients. Charging clients needs to be done systematically (versus the current ad-hoc system that many practices currently use).

2. Generate an extra $30,000 - $100,000 in fees in the first year

A good first-year target is $30,000 in tax planning revenue. The objective is for advisory services (tax planning and business advisory) to grow to 50% of a practice's revenue over time. For some practices, achieving this target will increase their fees by 100%.

3. Tax planning price list

The **minimum prices** to be charged are:

Individual clients (simple affairs)	$750 + GST
Individual clients (complex affairs)	$1,100 + GST
Small business (up to $200,000 turnover)	$1,000 - $1,500 + GST
Medium business ($200,001 to $500,000 turn-over)	$1,500 - $2,000 + GST
Large business ($500,001 to $1,500,000 turnover)	$2,000 + GST
Large business ($1,500,001 to $3,000,000 turn-over)	$3,000 + GST
Large business ($3,000,001 or more turnover)	$5,000 + GST
Tax scenario comparison (up to 5 scenarios)	$500 + GST
Professional firm profit allocation PCG 2021/4)	$750 + GST

The tax planning services price list can be provided to employees and clients.

4. Pricing systems/basis

- Cost-based pricing
- Value-based pricing
- Competitor-based pricing (What competitors?)
- Dynamic pricing
- Tiered or subscription pricing
- Psychological pricing
- Outcome-based/performance pricing

5. Why value-based pricing is best for tax planning and business advisory

- Reflects the client's financial benefit.
- Unlocks higher revenue potential.
- Positions you as a strategic advisor, not a technician
- Clients understand they are getting a result, not just hours.
- Positions you as a strategic advisor.
- Incentivises efficiency and innovation.
- Aligns your interests with the clients.
- Supports scalable advisory services

6. Fee fundamentals

Key points to remember:

- Free advice and complimentary services are not worth anything. The client knows it, and you know it. Any time an accountant provides a free service to a client, they tell the client, I haven't done my job correctly, I couldn't be bothered making an effort, and I know what I provided is worthless to you, so it's free.
- Tax planning is a high-value specialist service and is not a free service to be bundled in with the compliance service fee (for the same reasons as detailed above).
- Under no circumstances should clients be charged less than the minimum fees detailed in section 7.3.
- Tax planning is not the same as compliance. Tax planning involves specific skills and expertise, study, and training - it is a specialist service. Therefore, it should have a much higher effective hourly rate than standard compliance services, which can be obtained widely throughout the industry as a general service.
- As your tax planning experience, confidence, and expertise grow, you will add more value to clients. This will enable

you to increase your fees to 2-3 times the minimum fees detailed in section 7.3.

- Clients of professional services firms associate bigger bills with better value and higher quality services. Beaton Research and Consulting's annual professional services survey found an important correlation between fee levels and perceived quality.

This is known as the 'designer handbag effect'. Shoppers expect the most premium designer handbags to cost thousands of dollars – a hefty price tag signals these goods are the 'real deal' and top quality. The association between price and perceived quality has been found to apply to all industries.

7. Pyschology of pricing

Price the outcome, not the time	Use a tiered pricing model	Demonstrate ROI and user case studies	Offer fixed fees, not hourly rates	Position as an investment, not a cost

Use scarcity and exclusivity	Offer payment options

8. Example – pricing table for a practice

Service tier	Price (ex GST)	Value proposition
Tax optimiser	$2,000	Basic tax plan + compliance alignment
Wealth builder	$3,300	Full tax plan + profit benchmarks + trust strategy
Legacy planner	$9,900	Strategic plan + restructuring + asset protection + SMSF + advisory

Step 4 – Educate clients

'GIVE A MAN A FISH AND YOU FEED HIM FOR A DAY, TEACH A
MAN TO FISH AND YOU FEED HIM FOR A LIFETIME'
– MAIMONIDES (SPANISH – PHILOSOPHER, 1135-1204).

You are at STEP 4

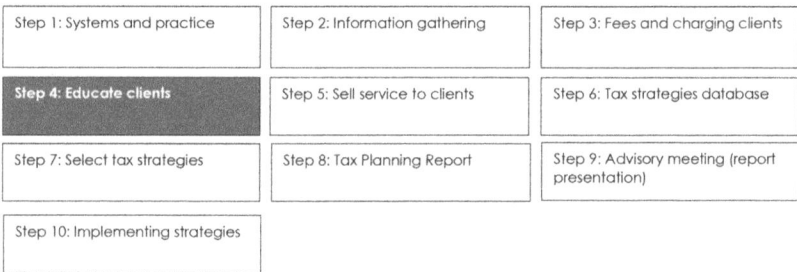

Step 1: Systems and practice	Step 2: Information gathering	Step 3: Fees and charging clients
Step 4: Educate clients	Step 5: Sell service to clients	Step 6: Tax strategies database
Step 7: Select tax strategies	Step 8: Tax Planning Report	Step 9: Advisory meeting (report presentation)
Step 10: Implementing strategies		

1. The objective of client education

Step 4 of the tax planning process is to 'educate clients'. The objective is to educate taxpayers on:

- What tax planning includes.
- Their opportunities to save tax.
- Their tax situation (i.e. taxable income, tax expense, tax paid, and tax owing/refundable for each group member for the current financial year).
- Their financial position, i.e. net worth (assets and liabilities).
- Tax planning in general (i.e. what it is, how it works, and who does it).

The benefits of educating your clients include:

- Generates extra fees/revenue. If you show clients how tax planning works and the opportunities for them to save tax, a large percentage will use tax planning services.
- Demonstrates your knowledge and expertise. This provides concrete evidence that you are an 'expert', which is essential as it aids client retention and generates referrals to help grow your business.
- It improves their financial literacy and helps them run a better business.
- Builds trust and helps you develop a deeper level of engagement with them.

2. What tax planning includes

1. Wealth creation (business and/or investments).
2. Saving future tax (before retirement).
3. Saving future tax (after retirement).
4. CGT on business and personal assets.
5. Ensuring tax compliance.
6. Resolving tax-related issues, i.e. Div 7a loans.
7. Forecasting tax liabilities.
8. Ensuring cash flow is available for a tax payment schedule.
9. Wealth and asset structures.
10. Saving stamp duty, payroll tax, and land tax.
11. Saving tax – prior to 30th June.

3. Three compliance quality control checklists

In **section 5.2** we discussed the benefits of fully integrating tax planning services into your practice. An easy first step is to include the three quality control checklists in your compliance delivery process.

The three quality control checklists are:
- Business quality control checklist.
- BAS quality control checklist.
- Individual quality control checklist.

We recommend that the quality control checklists be provided to all clients when their compliance service is completed. This can be at the client meeting for discussion and signing, or when the documents are emailed to clients for signing. The benefits of this are two-fold:
- Reinforces to the the client the process and work undertaken to provide compliance services (tax return, financial statements and BAS). Clients generally have no idea what accountants actually do for them as they only see the final product or outcome (e.g. tax return).
- Puts the client 'wants' questions in front of the client (up to five times per year for business clients). This non-intrusive repetition gets the client thinking about what's important to them.

4. Educational brochures

The brochures educate clients with no work effort, apply repetition and are free. The three brochures are:
- Why your business needs tax planning?
- Tax planning process).
- Why your business needs business advisory.

The three brochures should be used in the following ways:
- Colour printed and placed in reception and visible to clients (so they can take if interested).
- If a client starts talking about paying too much tax or asks what can be done, then hand the tax planning process brochure to them and discuss.

- If a client starts talking about how their business is struggling or performance/operational issues exist, then hand them the business advisory brochure and discuss.

5. Apply repetition

As consumers, advertising or marketing clutter surrounds us, and we are exposed to large volumes of advertising messages daily. We went from exposure of 500 ads in the 1970s to as many as 10,000 a day today. This phenomenon results from an overcrowded marketplace with products, leading to huge customer competition.

This is evident in the accounting industry, which has over 800 different products/services being marketed/sold to accounting practices to help them generate revenue, cut costs, improve productivity and market themselves.

Effectively educating taxpayers in this super-saturated world requires repetition.

Microsoft did a study to investigate the optimal number of exposures required for audio messages and concluded between 6 and 20 was best.

'The Rule of Seven' is an old marketing adage that says a potential customer needs to see or hear your marketing message at least seven times before they take action and buy from you. You can't just engage in a marketing activity once and then be done.

In 1885 Thomas Smith wrote a guide called 'Success Advertising' which stated:
- The 1st time people look at any given ad, they don't even see it.
- The 2nd time, they don't notice it.
- The 3rd time, they are aware that it is there.
- The 4th time, they have a fleeting sense that they've seen it somewhere before.

- The 5th **time**, they actually read the ad.
- The 6th **time**, they thumb their nose at it.
- The 7th **time**, they start to get a little irritated with it.
- The 8th **time**, they start to think, 'Here's that confounded ad again.'
- The 9th **time**, they start to wonder if they're missing out on something.
- The 10th **time**, they ask their friends and neighbours if they've tried it.
- The 11th **time**, they wonder how the company is paying for all these ads.
- The 12th **time**, they start to think that it must be a good product.
- The 13th **time**, they start to feel the product has value.
- The 14th **time**, they start to remember wanting a product exactly like this for a long time.
- The 15th **time**, they start to yearn for it because they can't afford to buy it.
- The 16th **time**, they accept the fact that they will buy it sometime in the future.
- The 17th **time**, they make a note to buy the product.
- The 18th **time**, they curse their poverty for not allowing them to buy this terrific product.
- The 19th **time**, they count their money very carefully.
- The 20th **time** they see the ad, they buy what is offering.

So why do your clients need to hear your message many times before taking action?

- Noise – there are too many messages, and too many are complete BS.
- They don't need you yet, or the time is not right for them.
- They're worried about the price.

- They don't know, like or trust you – basically, they don't believe you can deliver the promised benefits/results.

Effective frequency teaches that advertising and branding must be repetitive to achieve results. This means potential customers see the advertisements seven, ten, or twenty times. Research shows that the more repetition over a longer period, the better the long-term results.

McDonald's has been advertising on Australian TV daily for **thirty years.**

6. Top 8 repetition-based marketing strategies for selling tax planning and business advisory services

1. Monthly email campaigns (educational/value-based)	➤ Send 1 email per month with a **tax-saving tip, case study**, or **advisory insight**. ➤ Use subject lines like:Tax tips • "How a $3,600 strategy saved $22,000 in tax." • "The 4 biggest tax planning mistakes in 2025."
2. Social media drip campaigns (2x per week)	➤ Post consistently to LinkedIn, Facebook, and Instagram using: • Tax tips • Client results • Business benchmarking insights • Short videos
3. Quarterly webinars (live or on-demand)	➤ Topics like "Top 10 Tax Planning Strategies for Business Owners" ➤ Include a soft call-to-action to book an advisory session
4. Monthly client newsletter	➤ Send to all current clients—even those not yet doing advisory. ➤ Include a "Featured Strategy of the Month" or benchmarking success story.
5. In-office posters and table cards	➤ Display advisory success stories, benchmarking charts, "Ask us how to reduce your tax by 25%" ➤ Even returning clients see the message multiple times.

6. Repetition at key times in the year	➤ **Pre-June 30:** Urgency to save tax now ➤ **July–August:** Planning for new financial year ➤ **November:** Strategy reviews ➤ **February:** Trust distributions and restructure planning

7. Sales scripts that reinforce value repeatedly	➤ During consultations, repeat phrases like:
	  • "This strategy typically saves our clients $10,000–$20,000"
	  • "Many of our clients saw 2x their advisory fee in savings"

8. Follow-up calls and check-ins (every 60–90 days)	➤ Systemised calls or emails to follow up with:
	  • Previous prospects
	  • Clients who said "not now"
	  • Businesses you've already done tax returns for

7. Educate every client

Don't prejudge clients and only educate the ones you think will be interested in a particular subject/service. Instead, all clients should be treated equally and allowed to be educated (if they desire). Even if a subject/service is not of interest to a particular client now (say they are a salary return client), remember that their future circumstances can change (i.e. they could start a business).

In addition, no client is an island. They all have family, friends, and work colleagues who are all potential practice clients. Don't miss the opportunity to indirectly market to these potential clients.

8. Automate the process

Too many accountants market only sporadically because they are 'too busy' to market themselves. Then, they wonder why they don't have enough clients or are not growing fast enough. The solution to this problem is to automate the process so you are engaging in marketing (client education) activities, even when you're busy.

Sections 5.2 and 5.4 explain how to integrate the process of educating clients.

9

Step 5 - Sell service to client

'EVERYONE LIVES BY SELLING SOMETHING'
– ROBERT LOUISE STEVENSON (SCOTTISH WRITER, 1850 – 1894).

You are at STEP 5

Step 1: Systems and practice	Step 2: Information gathering	Step 3: Fees and charging clients
Step 4: Educate clients	**Step 5: Sell service to clients**	Step 6: Tax strategies database
Step 7: Select tax strategies	Step 8: Tax Planning Report	Step 9: Advisory meeting (report presentation)
Step 10: Implementing strategies		

1. Seven key steps for maintaining a positive mindset when selling

- Believe in the value you offer
- Focus on helping, not selling
- Reframe rejection
- Prepare and practice
- Celebrate small wins
- Stay energised and curious
- Focus on the process – not individual results

2. TaxFitness selling system

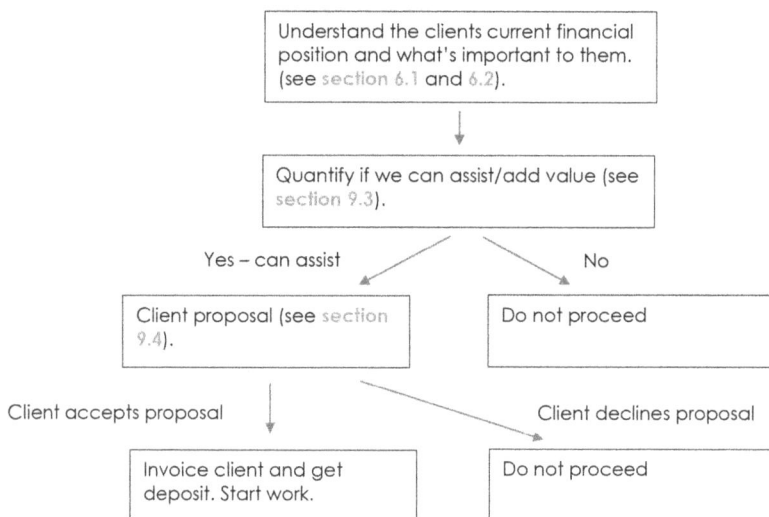

```
┌─────────────────────────────────────────┐
│ Understand the clients current financial  │
│ position and what's important to them.    │
│ (see section 6.1 and 6.2).                │
└─────────────────────────────────────────┘
                    │
                    ▼
┌─────────────────────────────────────────┐
│ Quantify if we can assist/add value (see  │
│ section 9.3).                             │
└─────────────────────────────────────────┘
```

Yes – can assist   No

```
┌──────────────────────────┐   ┌──────────────────────────┐
│ Client proposal (see section │   │ Do not proceed           │
│ 9.4).                      │   │                          │
└──────────────────────────┘   └──────────────────────────┘
```

Client accepts proposal   Client declines proposal

```
┌──────────────────────────┐   ┌──────────────────────────┐
│ Invoice client and get     │   │ Do not proceed           │
│ deposit. Start work.       │   │                          │
└──────────────────────────┘   └──────────────────────────┘
```

3. Quantify if we can assist and add value

Our first task is to understand the client's current financial position and what's important to them (see **section 6.1** and **6.2**). Secondly, we need to quantify if we can assist and add value.

Using the information collected in the interview checklist, plus other known client information, we need to:

- Determine how we can assist the client to achieve their 'wants.
- Quantify the benefits/value we can add, e.g. $20,000 tax savings this year, protect assets, eliminate CGT on future business sale, etc.
- Quantify how long it will take us to provide the service and what the fee should be.

If we can assist and add value to the client at least 3 times our fee/cost (ideally 5 to 10 times), then we proceed to the client proposal. If we cannot achieve this return on investment for the client, we don't proceed to the client proposal stage.

4. Client proposal

Articulate quantified benefits/value

Explain process

Fees and credit terms

Ask the client if they want to proceed.

Email

Client meeting, discussions

Phone call

5. What tax planning services can you sell to your clients?

The tax planning services include tax planning reports, client meetings and report discussions and implementation.

The services price list **starting from** fees are:

Individual clients (simple affairs)	$750 + GST
Individual clients (complex affairs)	$1,100 + GST
Small business (up to $200,000 turnover)	$1,100 - $1,500 + GST
Medium business ($200,001 to $500,000 turnover)	$1,500 - $2,000 + GST
Large business ($500,001 to $1,500,000 turnover)	$2,000 + GST
Large business ($1,500,001 to $3,000,000 turnover)	$3,000 + GST
Large business ($3,000,001 or more turnover)	$5,000 + GST
Tax scenario comparison (up to 5 scenarios)	$500 + GST
Professional firm profit allocation PCG 2021/4)	$750 + GST

The tax planning services price list can be provided to employees and clients. For further information on fees and charging clients see **Chapter 7**.

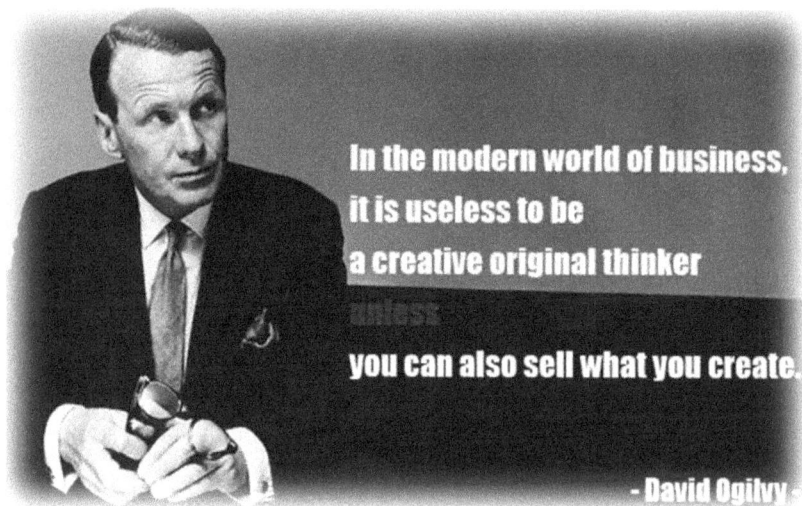

In the modern world of business, it is useless to be a creative original thinker unless you can also sell what you create.

– David Ogilvy

6. Focus on existing clients – not new clients.

When selling the service to clients, we must focus our attention, time, and energy on our existing clients, not on chasing new ones. Research confirms this produces the optimum results because:

- The probability of selling to an existing customer is 60-70%, while the probability of selling to a new prospect is 5%-20%.
- Existing customers are 50% more likely to try new products and spend 31% more than new customers.
- It costs five times more to attract a new customer than to keep an existing one.
- Increasing customer retention rates by 5% increases profits by 25% to 95%.

If we can assist the clients to achieve their 'wants'/goal and quantify the benefits that can be achieved and they can receive a 3/1 return on investment, our conversion rate will be 90%+.

7. Work the percentages

As discussed above, research shows the probability of selling to an existing client is 60-70%. If you follow the TaxFitness selling system it will be 90%+. As the figure is not 100%, it is clear that not every existing client will buy every new product or service you offer them.

When working the percentages, a few things to remember:

- For optimum results, consistently follow the process detailed in this chapter. Use the same process every time; consistency is everything.
- As it will take time to develop your selling skills, confidence, and expertise, a 75% success rate for the first 12 months is realistic.
- Over time, your success rate in selling to clients will rise to 90%+.
- The more clients you present to and follow the process with, the more successful you will be. This means, for example, that you want to follow the process with 100 clients per year, not 10. There is a big difference between the fees generated from 50 tax planning reports compared to 5.
- Don't take 'no' responses personally. The client may just not be interested, or it may not be the right time for them – you can do nothing about those things.

10.

Step 6 – Tax strategies database

AN INVESTMENT IN KNOWLEDGE PAYS THE BEST INTEREST'
– BENJAMIN FRANKLIN (AMERICAN POLITICIAN, 1706 – 1790).

You are at STEP 6

Step 1: Systems and practice	Step 2: Information gathering	Step 3: Fees and charging clients
Step 4: Educate clients	Step 5: Sell service to clients	**Step 6: Tax strategies database**
Step 7: Select tax strategies	Step 8: Tax Planning Report	Step 9: Advisory meeting (report presentation)
Step 10: Implementing strategies		

1. Intellectual property and know-how

Step 6 of the tax planning process is the tax strategies database. This intellectual property and know-how is the foundation of the tax planning process. The TaxFitness database includes:

- Tax strategies: 200+.
- ATO obligations: 18.
- Business structures: 38.
- Recommendations: 64.
- Consistent weekly upgrades and maintenance to include tax law changes.
- TaxFitness business advisory database: 350+.
- TaxFitness business benchmarks: 400+.

2. Tax strategies structure

In the TaxFitness database, each strategy has been divided into four sections:

Section		Explanation
1	Implementation advice (of the strategy).	The '**Implementation advice**' explains the step-by-step process for legally and effectively implementing each strategy. Following the implementation process and completing the relevant paperwork is essential to obtaining the tax deduction. In addition, the estimated costs involved in implementing each strategy are detailed.
2	Strategy explanation.	The '**strategy explanation**' clearly explains the strategy so you can fully understand its background and how the tax savings are generated.
3	Deductions (average tax deductions).	The '**deductions**' for each strategy are the estimated tax deductions if the strategy were implemented.
4	Notes for the accountant.	The '**notes for the accountant**' section includes additional information the accountant needs to consider.

3. Tax strategy attributes and attractiveness

Each tax strategy within the database has **five main attributes**:

- Type of taxpayer it applies to.
- Implementation process and costs.
- Deductions size (average).
- One-off or ongoing tax deductions.
- Capital investment component.

The **five types of taxpayers** (or taxpayer circumstances) are:

- Business,
- Investors and retirees,
- Employees,
- Rental properties,
- SMSF.

Factors that make one tax strategy more attractive than others:

- **The strategies are refined.** Some tax strategies only apply to one type of taxpayer. The tax strategy, 'employing the family', for example, only applies to businesses. Other tax strategies are more versatile and can equally apply to business owners, investors and employees. The 'negative gearing' tax strategy is a perfect example of this.
- **Size of deductions.** All things being equal, a tax strategy with larger deductions will be more attractive than a smaller deduction. For example, the tax strategy where an employee's salary package for their private motor vehicle (a $9,000 deduction) is more attractive than the one for protective clothing (a $200 deduction).
- **One-off or ongoing.** The tax deductions generated from a particular tax strategy can be one-off or ongoing. All things being equal, a tax strategy producing ongoing annual tax deductions will be more attractive than one with a once-off tax deduction.

- **Twin objectives.** Tax strategies with a capital investment component simultaneously achieve the twin objectives of tax deductions (and saving tax) and investment. The pros are obvious; tax-deductible (and save tax), plus make an investment (that will hopefully exceed the initial cash outflows and continue to grow in value over time). Taxpayers love these investments with a passion and this is evidenced by the 2 million taxpayers owning a negatively geared rental property.
- **The implementation costs for a tax strategy are the additional costs incurred on top of the standard cost of the deduction.** For most strategies the standard cost of the deduction and the average tax deduction are equal. For example, $20,000 employer super contributions will create a $20,000 tax deduction. In this super contribution's example, there are no extra implementation costs.
- **Ideal tax strategies are those few strategies that can provide a tax deduction with no standard cost outlay.** The 2.5% building write-off on rental properties is a good example of this as the average tax deduction is $10,000 with $0 standard cost.
- **The implementation process and costs for individual tax strategies vary from one extreme to another.** Ideal tax planning strategies have nil costs and are simple and quick to implement. Other strategies can involve high costs and long implementation processes. For example, the sale of a commercial property by a company to the business owner's SMSF will involve stamp duty ($50,000), solicitor's fees for the sale (several thousand dollars), and three months. Despite these high costs, this strategy is still highly beneficial as the annual tax savings can recoup these costs within three years, and the tax savings could be ongoing for thirty years.

4. TaxFitness 'Tax Strategy Database'

The current TaxFitness tax strategy database is below. The most popular strategies are found at 1 – 59.

List of TaxFitness Tax Strategies	
No.	**Strategy Title**
1	$20,000 instant asset write-off
2	5-year catch-up super contributions
3	Add holding company to trading company
4	Bucket companies
5	Business registrations
6	Change bad debt to good debt
7	Change from employee to contractor
8	Change ownership of assets
9	Child maintenance trust
10	Companies I
11	Computers, tools, equipment and other assets
12	Concessional superannuation contributions
13	Debt recycling
14	Discretionary trust
15	Dividend deductions
16	Double dip for employees claiming motor vehicle expenses reimbursed by their employees
17	Electric cars are FBT free
18	Eliminate Division 7A loans
19	Employee meals on business premises
20	FBT exemptions and reductions
21	FBT obligations
22	Five-year rule for new residential premises
23	Fuel tax credits
24	Fully maintained associate lease
25	Granny flats
26	GST obligations

27	Income tax
28	Jointly owned motor vehicles
29	Life insurance held through superannuation
30	Margin scheme
31	Negatively geared rental property
32	Negatively geared share portfolio
33	Negatively gearing the family home
34	Overseas super transfer
35	PAYG withholding obligations
36	Payroll tax
37	Pedigree tax
38	Property depreciation reports
39	Property related transactions
40	PSI entity
41	Pty Ltd with family trust as shareholders
42	Record keeping – ATO
43	Refinancing the family home
44	Salary packaging private motor vehicles
45	Self-managed super fund borrowings
46	Share trader v share investor
47	SMSF's investing in non-controlled entities
48	Start a pension in a SMSF (or zero tax retirement)
49	Super contributions from downsizing
50	Super withdrawal and contribution strategy
51	Superannuation and SMSFs
52	Superannuation guarantee
53	Taxable payments reporting
54	Transfer personal investments into super
55	Transferring business premises into a SMSF
56	Transition to retirement pensions
57	Transporting heavy or bulky equipment
58	Unit trust
59	Using a SMSF to undertake a property development

60	$1,000 in-house benefits
61	15 year small business CGT exemption
62	30th June trust distribution minutes
63	Accelerated depreciation for farmers
64	Accessing surplus franking accounts
65	Accommodation and meals at remote sites
66	Accrued directors' fee
67	Accrued expenses
68	Active assets indefinitely
69	Airport lounge memberships
70	All-inclusive holiday package
71	Allocating the purchase price of business assets acquired
72	Antique, veteran or vintage car
73	Art
74	Asset protection
75	ATO payment plan
76	Auto-reversionary pension
77	Avoid underpaying employees
78	Bad debts
79	Benchmarking
80	Binding death benefit nominations
81	Blackhole expenditure
82	Boats and yachts
83	Bona fide travel allowance
84	Budgeting
85	Build-to-rent developments
86	Business digital adoption
87	Business exit planning
88	Business insurance – the essentials
89	Business plan
90	Business saleability
91	Business valuation
92	Business value improvement

93	Buy your business premises
94	Cash flow statement
95	Cash 'v' accrual accounting methods
96	Change a hobby into a business
97	Change PSI into business income
98	Change PSI to personal services business (PSB)
99	Changing effective life of depreciating assets
100	Charitable trust
101	Christmas party
102	Cloud accounting software
103	Clubs, societies and other associations
104	Company deregistration
105	Compliance audit of ATO obligations
106	Compulsory work uniform
107	Consumer protection
108	Corporate box
109	Cryptocurrencies
110	Crystallise capital losses
111	Customer disputed amounts
112	Debtor management
113	Deceased estates taxed under s99
114	Delay income and the realisation of assets
115	Departing Australia superannuation payment
116	Deregistered company
117	Digital games tax offset
118	Director penalty notices
119	Directors' duties and the Corporations Act 2001
120	Div 7A loan agreement
121	Division 43
122	Divorcing spouses' CGT asset rollover
123	Donations
124	Double tax agreement
125	Doubler the deductible super contributions limit

126	Early-stage innovation company
127	Electric vehicle home charging expenses
128	Eligible start-up costs
129	Eliminate DIV 293 tax
130	Employee remuneration trusts
131	Employee share schemes
132	Employees of religious institutions
133	Employing the family
134	Employment agreements
135	Entertainment
136	Entertainment facility leasing expenses
137	Environmental protection activities
137	Establish a family SMSF
139	Establish a not-for-profit company
140	Excess concessional super contributions
141	Exempt childcare benefits
142	Export market development grant
143	External training expenditure
144	Family trust distribution to adult children
145	Family trust election
146	Family discretionary trust
147	Farm management deposits
148	FBT exempt work-related items
149	Finance with 100% overseas debt
150	Financial planner advise
151	First home super saver scheme
152	Fitness expenses
153	Four-year construction rule
154	Fuel efficient luxury cars
155	Full commutation of a TRIS
156	General pool balance less than $20,000
157	Genuine redundancy payments
158	Gifts to clients, suppliers and contractors

159	GST going concern exemption
160	Handbags, briefcases and satchels
161	Health coaching, lifestyle and weight-loss
162	Holding companies
163	Holiday homes
164	Home-based businesses
165	Home office fixed rate method
166	Home office occupancy expenses
167	Home to work travel
168	Husband and wife partnerships
169	Implementation fees
170	Income protection insurance
171	Income protection insurance: benefits
172	Incorporated association
173	Increasing giving via discretionary trusts
174	In-house recreation facilities
175	Intangible depreciating assets
176	Interest deductions for rental properties
177	Internal controls
178	Invest to save tax
179	Investment bonds
180	Itinerant travel
181	Joint venture
182	Keep everything legal
183	Land tax
184	Legal expenses
185	Life insurance
186	Liquidate company
187	Living away from home allowance (LAFHA)
188	Logbook for motor vehicles
189	Long service awards
190	Long service leave
191	Long-term goals

192	Luxury car leases
193	Main residence 6-month rule
194	Main residence exemption
195	Making holidays deductible
196	Management fees
197	Managing tax affairs
198	Maximising the $1.9m pension cap
199	Migrant language training
200	Minimum pension payments
201	Mortgage offset account
202	Motor vehicle expenses: cents per km method
203	New energy incentive
204	Non-geared unit trusts
205	Notifiable data breaches scheme
206	Novated motor vehicle lease
207	Occupational health and counselling
208	On the 1st July 2024 individual tax rates are reduced
209	Outsourced CFO
210	Overnight travel expenses
211	Overseas conferences, courses and study tours
212	Overtime meal expenses
213	Partnership of discretionary trusts
214	Partnerships
215	Passing the non-commercial loss rules
216	Passively-held assets: Small business CGT concessions
217	Pay a dividend
218	Pay wages to directors or trustees
219	Pets in the workplace
220	Phone and internet
221	Prepaid income – Arthur Murray case
222	Prepay accounting fees
223	Prepayment deductions
224	Primary producer tax averaging

225	Primary production business
226	Privacy & data protection
227	Private investment companies
228	Professional practice company
229	Profit and loss budget
230	Profit improvement
231	Property seminars
232	Proprietary limited company (limited by shares)
233	Protect intellectual property
234	Protective clothing
235	Purchase a farm in your SMSF
236	Quarterly accountant review & meeting
237	Reducing super guarantee payments
238	Refund of Division 293 tax for temporary residents permanently leaving Australia
239	Releasing trapped company franking credits
240	Relocation expenses
241	Remote area housing benefits
242	Rental property repairs
243	Research and development
244	Retirement exemption – CGT concession for small business
245	Retraining and reskilling staff
246	Review business structures
247	Risk management: business
248	Risk management: individuals
249	Rollover from sole trader to company
250	Safety award
251	Salary packaging associated leases
252	Salary packaging for FBT rebatable employees
253	Salary packaging for FBT-exempt employees
254	Salary packaging rental and share investment losses to 'beat' the income test rules

255	Salary packaging rental property expenses to double dip and save the GST
256	School building fund levy
257	Secret trust
258	Self-education expenses
259	Self-audit FBT obligations
260	Self-development courses and seminars
261	Sell a business and pay no tax
262	Service arrangement
263	Service trust
264	Share buybacks
265	Share investment seminars
266	Shareholder agreements
267	Short-term goals
268	Small business CGT rollover
269	Small business restructure roll-over
270	Small businesses' top 20 tax compliance issues
271	Smartwatch
272	SMSF
273	SMSF bare trust
274	SMSF carrying on a business
275	Sole trader
276	Solvency resolutions: companies
277	Special disability trust
278	Sponsorship
279	Spouse super contributions
280	Streaming trust income
281	Succession planning
282	Sunglasses, sunscreens and cosmetics
283	Super fund trustee company
284	Tax consolidation
285	Tax deductible dogs
286	Tax incentive for early-stage investors

287	Taxi, uber and ride-share travel
288	Temporary absence rule
289	Temporary residents
290	Testamentary trust
291	Travel between two unrelated places of employment
292	Travel to a tax agent
293	Trust closure and vesting
294	Trust resolution. No streaming
295	Trust resolution. Streaming
296	Trustee company
297	Union fees, licences, registrations and subscriptions
298	Update SMSF deed
299	Update trust deeds
300	Utilise business goodwill to pay out your private mortgage
301	Valuing trading stock
302	Varying partners distributions
303	Voluntary bankruptcy
304	Wealth creation
305	Workers compensation insurance
306	Workplace health safety (WHS) laws
307	X-box, Foxtel and pinball machines

5. Knowing your A, B, C's

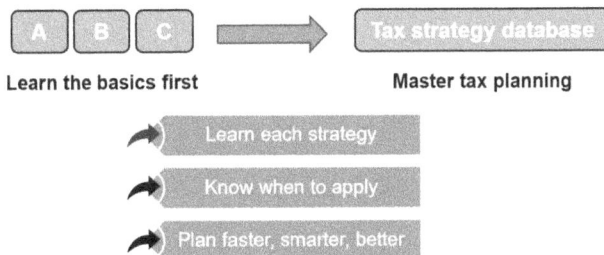

A B C ⟶ Tax strategy database

Learn the basics first   Master tax planning

Learn each strategy

Know when to apply

Plan faster, smarter, better

**"No shortcuts. Learn the strategies.
Master the outcomes."**

11.

Step 7 - Select tax strategies

'THERE IS NO GREAT GENIUS WITHOUT
SOME TOUCH OF MADNESS'
– ARISTOTLE (GREEK PHILOSOPHER, 384 BC – 322 BC).

You are at STEP 7

Step 1: Systems and practice	Step 2: Information gathering	Step 3: Fees and charging clients
Step 4: Educate clients	Step 5: Sell service to clients	Step 6: Tax strategies database
Step 7: Select tax strategies	Step 8: Tax Planning Report	Step 9: Advisory meeting (report presentation)
Step 10: Implementing strategies		

1. Key steps in strategy selection

- **Understand the client:** Income, assets, structures, goals.
- **Identify strategy categories:** Income, entity, investment, timing, super.
- **Shortlist strategies:** Fit client, compliant, beneficial.
- **Evaluate impact:** Tax savings, costs, risks.
- **Prioritise:** Best outcomes, easy wins, urgency.
- **Propose and discuss:** Clear explanation, benefits, risks.
- **Implement:** Action plan and monitor progress.

2. Why one strategy would be more attractive than others

1. Financial impact
2. Ease of implementation
3. Eligibility and timing
4. Cost to benefit ratio
5. Strategic alignment
6. Simplicity
7. Psychological comfort
8. ATO acceptance

3. Thirteen 'Golden Rules' for selecting tax strategies for a client

1. **Understand the client**
   (Deep dive into financial position and goals.)
2. **Commercial purpose first**
   (Ensure genuine business or investment intent.)
3. **Align with client goals**
   (Match strategies to personal and business objectives.)
4. **Only 1 – 10 tax strategies**
   (Avoid information overload.)
5. **Select low-hanging fruit first**
   (Get early wins on board with client.)
6. **Timing is critical**
   (Implement early to maximise benefits.)
7. **Focus on long-term benefits**
   (Seek sustainable, compounding advantages.)
8. **Balance risk and reward**
   (Choose strategies with strong compliance standing.)
9. **Use structures smartly**
   (Leverage companies, trusts, SMSFS where appropriate.)

10. **Maximise immediate deductions**
    (Prioritise strategies giving instant tax savings.)
11. **Layer strategies for impact**
    (Combine multiple strategies for stronger outcomes.)
12. **Keep it simple and defensible**
    (Choose clear, understandable, and compliant strategies.)
13. **It may take several drafts (Jeffery Archer – Author)**

4. Selecting tax strategies – manual 'v' AI

Manual (Traditional Selection)	TaxFitness AI (Smart Selection)
Slow and time-consuming *Manual research for each strategy.*	Instant recommendations *AI scans full strategy database instantly.*
Risk of missed strategies *Dependent on adviser memory/experience.*	Comprehensive coverage *Nothing overlooked, full system search.*
Inconsistent advice *Varies between advisers and cases.*	Consistent, reliable advice *Every client gets top-quality outcomes.*
Requires deep manual knowledge *High ongoing study load.*	Pre-trained, always updated *Strategy knowledge built-in.*
Not easily scalable *More clients = more adviser time.*	Highly scalable *More clients = no extra workload.*
Manual risk assessment *Time-consuming to check risks.*	Built-in risk profiling *Strategies ranked by risk level.*
Hard to combine strategies efficiently	Smart layering of strategies *Optimises outcomes.*
Manual documentation *Inconsistent ATO defence.*	Clear, structured documentation *ATO-ready.*
Slow client turnaround	Fast, professional client delivery

5. Human expertise + TaxFitness AI = Superior tax strategy selection

Understands client emotions, goals, and commercial realities	Rapid, full database search for all strategies
Applies professional judgment and practical wisdom	Ensures speed, consistency, and comprehensive coverage
Balances strategy risk, compliance, and practicality	Built-in risk scoring and audit defence documentation
Builds client relationships and trust	Frees time for higher-value client work

12.

Step 8 - Tax planning report

You are at STEP 8

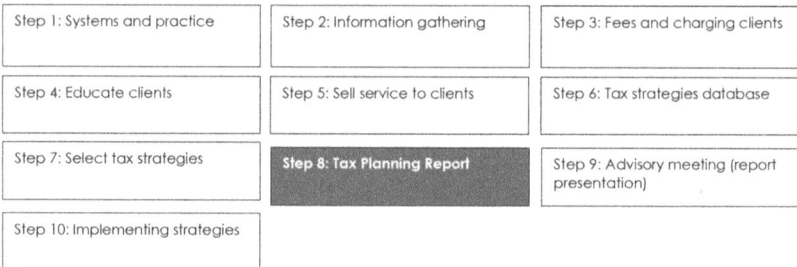

Step 1: Systems and practice	Step 2: Information gathering	Step 3: Fees and charging clients
Step 4: Educate clients	Step 5: Sell service to clients	Step 6: Tax strategies database
Step 7: Select tax strategies	**Step 8: Tax Planning Report**	Step 9: Advisory meeting (report presentation)
Step 10: Implementing strategies		

1. Purpose of the report

Step 8 of the tax planning process is the 'tax planning report'. The tax planning report has two functions:

- Show the tax currently being paid and highlight the potential tax savings.
- Explaining the selected tax strategies.

66

2. Tax planning with a report 'v' without a report

Tax Planning WITH a Report	Tax Planning WITHOUT a Report
Clear documentation and structure	No formal record of advice
Quantifies tax savings (real $ value)	Harder for clients to understand benefits
Enhances audit defence and compliance	Higher ATO audit and dispute risk
Builds client confidence and trust	Less professional — may damage perception
Justifies premium advisory fees	Difficult to charge high-value fees
Easier to implement and action strategies	Risk of client confusion or non-action
Strengthens client retention and referrals	Missed opportunities for engagement and growth

3. Purpose of the tax planning report

Identify tailored tax strategies	Personalised recommendations matched to the client's situation.
Quantify tax savings	Show clear, dollar-based savings estimates for each strategy.
Educate and empower clients	Explain strategies in simple, easy-to-understand language.
Provide an actionable plan	Logical, prioritised steps for fast implementation.
Enhance compliance and audit defence	Clear documentation to protect against ATO challenges.
Strengthen client engagement	Build deeper client trust and advisory loyalty.
Grow advisory revenue	Position tax planning as a premium, high-value service.

4. 10 keys to a superior tax planning report

	Key	Description
1.	Personalised advice	Tailor strategies to the client's unique situation — no generic templates.
2.	Quantify tax savings	Clearly show estimated savings ($) for each strategy and overall total.
3.	Logical structure	Present strategies in priority order based on impact and timing.
4.	Clear language	Use plain English — make the complex simple.
5.	Commercial purpose	Document business/commercial reasons, not just tax outcomes.
6.	Risk assessment	Include simple risk comments: Low, Medium, High.
7.	Practical action steps	Provide clear "What needs to be done" instructions.
8.	Professional presentation	Use neat tables, headings, and optional simple visuals.
9.	Consistency and compliance	Ensure language, structure, and compliance is tight and uniform.
10.	Executive summary	Start with a one-page high-level summary for quick decisions.

5. Why include and discuss recommendations

Reason	Description
Holistic advice	Advises on tax, business, risk, and wealth — not just tax returns.
Identify new opportunities	Spot gaps in risk management, insurance, structures, and planning.
Strengthen compliance	Protects clients from hidden legal, regulatory, and financial risks.
Differentiate your firm	Position as proactive, strategic and client-centric.
Grow advisory revenue	Each recommendation opens advisory project opportunities.
Protect the advisor	Document that broader risks and opportunities were raised professionally.
Support long-term retention	Clients stay longer when they see value beyond compliance services.

13.

Step 9 – Advisory meeting (report presentation)

'THE SINGLE BIGGEST PROBLEM IN COMMUNICATION IS THE ILLUSION IT HAS TAKEN PLACE'
– GEORGE BERNARD SHAW (IRISH DRAMATIST, 1856 – 1950).

You are at STEP 9

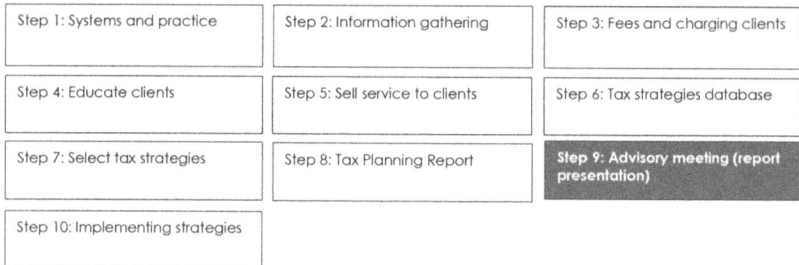

Step 1: Systems and practice	Step 2: Information gathering	Step 3: Fees and charging clients
Step 4: Educate clients	Step 5: Sell service to clients	Step 6: Tax strategies database
Step 7: Select tax strategies	Step 8: Tax Planning Report	**Step 9: Advisory meeting (report presentation)**
Step 10: Implementing strategies		

1. The objective - purpose

Step 9 of the tax planning process is an advisory meeting (report presentation). The objective of this step is for the client to understand the tax planning report and their options to save tax.

2. Advisory meeting - how to structure for optimal results

Function	Description
Present the report	Walk through strategies, savings, and recommendations.
Simplify the complex	Translate technical advice into plain English.
Prioritise and plan	Help the client focus on key strategies and next steps.
Educate and empower	Build client understanding and confidence to act.
Strengthen compliance	Document advice, commercial purpose, and informed choices.
Expand advisory opportunities	Introduce additional services like asset protection, business planning, and wealth creation.
Deliver a high-value experience	

3. Advisory meeting structure – lock in annual service

Step	Purpose
1. Prepare thoroughly	Review report, tailor strategies, and plan agenda.
2. Set the agenda early	Explain the meeting flow and manage expectations.
3. Present the report clearly	Walk through the Executive Summary, then each strategy in plain English.
4. Prioritise key strategies	Collaborate with the client on which actions to implement first.
5. Handle questions and concerns	Encourage discussion, overcome objections, simplify where needed.
6. Finalise the action plan	Confirm agreed strategies, who does what, and deadlines.
7. Introduce ongoing advisory	Position future meetings, reviews, and broader advisory services.
8. Close strong	Summarise wins, confirm next steps, and finish positively.

14.

Step 10 – Implementing strategies

You are at STEP 10

Step 1: Systems and practice	Step 2: Information gathering	Step 3: Fees and charging clients
Step 4: Educate clients	Step 5: Sell service to clients	Step 6: Tax strategies database
Step 7: Select tax strategies	Step 8: Tax Planning Report	Step 9: Advisory meeting (report presentation)
Step 10: Implementing strategies		

1. The objective

Step 10 of the tax planning process is 'Implementing strategies.
Without implementing the tax strategies, no tax will be saved.

2. Implementation options

Objective	Description
Execute the strategies	Turn the tax plan from theory into real-world actions.
Maximise tax savings	Deliver the financial benefits identified in the report.
Meet critical deadlines	Action timing-sensitive strategies (e.g., before 30 June).
Protect compliance and reduce risk	Ensure full, correct, and defensible implementation.
Strengthen client trust	Show you deliver on promises — building loyalty and credibility.
Document actions clearly	

3. Implementing strategies – client 'v' accountant 'v' combined

Who Implements	Advantages	Disadvantages
Client	• Lower cost • Greater ownership • Immediate action on simple tasks	• Risk of mistake • Missed deadlines • Poor compliance documentation
Accountant	• Professional, accurate execution • Full compliance and audit protection • Maximises tax savings	• Higher cost • May need third-party coordination
Combined	• Best balance of cost and precision • Client empowered on simple tasks • Accountant ensures critical strategies are secure	• Needs clear responsibility allocation • Requires strong communication

15.

Keep everything legal

'THE JOURNEY OF ONE THOUSAND MILES BEGINS WITH ONE STEP'

– LAO TZU (CHINESE PHILOSOPHER, 600 BC).

1. Legal 'v' illegal tax-saving strategies

Paying our legal taxes is a small price for the benefits we enjoy in a privileged, prosperous, and safe society such as Australia. The great majority of taxpayers, both individuals and corporations, pay their taxes voluntarily and in accordance with the law.

This course is about maximising legal tax savings by ensuring 100% compliance with the law (and the spirit of the law). Complying with the law to minimise your taxes legally is not a moral issue and is encouraged by legislation and government policy. **The listing of Australia's 10 most expensive legal tax breaks (below) shows that the concessional taxation of super-annuation contributions is at number 3 (with an annual cost of $16.9 billion).** Taxpayers utilising this tax strategy are saving tax but benefiting society as they provide for their retirement (so they will not be drawing down the age pension in their retirement). This is the Government's policy, and it is working efficiently and achieving its objective. Although there is a short-term cost in tax forgone, the economic long-term benefits to society are clear and measurable.

2. Australia's ten most expensive legal tax breaks

The Commonwealth Treasury's 2016 Tax Expenditures Statement (published in January 2017) shows Australian's ten most expensive tax breaks are:

1. Main residence exemption from CGT: $61.5 billion.
2. Concessional taxation of superannuation earnings $16.9 billion.
3. Concessional taxation of superannuation contributions $16.9 billion.
4. CGT discount for individuals and trusts $9.6 billion.
5. GST exemption for fresh food $6.9 billion.
6. GST exemption for education $4.5 billion.
7. GST exemption for health services $4 billion.
8. GST exemption for financial services $3.9 billion.
9. Concessional taxation of termination benefits $2.6 billion.
10. Exemption from interest withholding tax on securities $2.3 billion.

3. Top 15 illegal tax-saving strategies

The top 15 illegal tax-saving strategies are:

- Illegal cash economy - The ATO estimates about 1.6 million businesses (mostly micro and small businesses with an annual turnover up to $15 million) operating across 233 industries are part of the illegal cash economy. Tax Justice Network spokesman, Mark Zirnsak, said the ATO's data was just the 'tip of the iceberg of shady employers who cheat their employees of the wages they are owed and cheat the community of the taxes that should be paid'.
- Employees or contractors not declaring cash wages.
- Not reporting capital gains on the sale of shares or property.
- Not declaring interest, dividend or rental income.

- Not declaring overseas income like wages, capital gains, rent, etc.
- Setting up bogus businesses, registering for GST, collecting the GST credits on false purchases, then disappearing.
- Using stolen TFNs, ABNs and bank accounts to deposit income (which is never declared to the ATO).
- Claiming private expenditure as a work deduction (like home-to-work travel, meals and entertainment).
- Filing a tax return on July 1st with inflated earnings and tax withholding, collecting their return 7 to 14 days later and leaving the country before their employer has filed with the ATO, and the data can be verified. Popular with some overseas students who are never coming back to Australia.
- Inflating business expenses by creating false receipts or claiming non-deductible expenses (like private holidays or private mortgage expenses).
- Claiming bogus business deductions for payments made to overseas entities they control for supposedly marketing or management services.
- Profit shifting – Where the prices paid between related parties for goods, services or use of assets are inflated above their true economic value so that profits are artificially moved between different jurisdictions.
- Treaty shopping – Where transactions are organised through intermediaries located in particular jurisdictions in order to obtain different treaty benefits without those intermediaries materially contributing to the transaction;
- Residency manipulation – Where individuals and legal entities attempt to present themselves as residents of a low tax jurisdiction, or of nowhere.
- Global tax evasion can also occur through the use of secrecy jurisdictions to hide or wash money or other assets.

4. Income tax general anti-avoidance rules

The general anti-avoidance rules contained in Part IVA of the Income Tax Assessment Act 1936 (Cth) ('Part IVA') may be applied by the Australian Taxation Office (ATO) to deny a taxpayer the tax benefit of a scheme they have entered into.

The key features of Part IVA include the following:
1. Is there a scheme?
2. Has a tax benefit been obtained?
3. What was the taxpayer's sole or dominant purpose?
4. What happens when Part IVA is applied?

1. Is there a scheme?

It is important to identify the scheme as it sets the framework for determining if a taxpayer has obtained a tax benefit in connection with the scheme and whether the dominant purpose of the taxpayer of entering into the scheme was to obtain the tax benefit. Part IVA provides a broad definition of 'scheme', which includes any agreement, arrangement, promise or undertaking, whether express or implied and whether or not enforceable.

2. What is the tax benefit?

A 'tax benefit' is defined in section 177C as an amount not included in assessable income, a deduction being claimed or a capital loss being incurred. Furthermore, section 177C specifies that a taxpayer will have obtained a tax benefit in connection with a scheme if the tax benefit would not have arisen if the scheme did not occur, or would reasonably not have arisen if the scheme did not occur.

3. What was the taxpayer's sole or dominant purpose?

It is necessary to determine whether a person entered into or carried out a scheme for the sole or dominant 'purpose' of obtaining a tax benefit. If obtaining a tax benefit is only an incidental purpose of entering into a scheme, then this is not sufficient for Part IVA to apply. Whilst a transaction may be entered into based on a rational commercial decision, this does not necessarily mean that the dominant purpose has not been established. A decision to enter into a transaction can be both commercially and tax-driven, but the relevant purpose will be the one that is the most influential, ruling or prevailing purpose. Therefore, it is very important to have proper documentary evidence to a taxpayer's defence of Part IVA.

4. What happens when Part IVA is applied?

Where it is determined that the taxpayer entered into a scheme to obtain a tax benefit the Commissioner of Taxation has a discretion under section 177F(1) to cancel the relevant tax benefit. When considering any proposed transactions, you must carefully consider the transaction's commercial and economic substance. In particular, you should ensure that this substance can be clearly demonstrated in a reasonable alternative scheme. Apart from the impact of Part IVA applying to 'reverse' the impact of any scheme, if it is applied, the ATO can also impose penalties of up to 50% of the tax payable.

16.

Tax planning mistakes

1. Overview of tax planning mistakes

Let's examine the seven tax planning mistakes. For each 'mistake,' there is a price to be paid: lost public practice revenue and profits and lower client satisfaction.

Seven Deadly Sins Wealth without work Pleasure without conscience Science without humanity Knowledge without character Politics without principle Commerce without morality Worship without sacrifice.

— *Mahatma Gandhi* —

The seven tax planning mistakes are:
1. Failing to offer tax planning services to every client.
2. Undercharging for tax planning.
3. Inadequate time spent on the tax planning process.
4. Failing to gather client information and data.

5. Inadequate tax strategies database.
6. Failing to provide the client with a written tax planning report.
7. Inadequate tax planning training.

These are explained below.

2. Number 1: Failing to offer tax planning services to every client

Even practices currently providing tax planning services have been reluctant to offer them to all clients. Instead, there has been the tendency to only offer it to a few selected clients that seem ideal tax planning candidates. This second-guessing of what clients want and don't want is under-servicing clients and costing the practice money. This is equivalent to your local Woolworths supermarket only promoting and selling Indian food products to Indians or German beer to Germans. This doesn't make any sense.

Once again, when accountants do this to their clients, it doesn't make any sense. This provides an opportunity for tax planning practices to increase their revenue dramatically. All they need to do is offer the tax planning service to 100% of their clients, and inevitably, the number of tax planning services sold must increase.

3. Number 2: Undercharging for tax planning

Some principals think telling clients to put more money into super is tax planning. Of course, contributing to superannuation is a good tax planning strategy, but this isn't providing tax planning services. As discussed in **Chapter 4**, the tax planning process is a ten-stage process involving more than providing advice on one (or several) tax strategies.

Within the 20% of practices providing tax planning services, over 50% are undercharging for their tax planning services. The fees charged for tax planning are affected by:

- The accountant's confidence levels.
- The accountant's skill levels and expertise.
- The size and profitability of the client.
- The accountant's sales skills.
- The value-added and tax saved by the accountant.

The problem with undercharging for the service is that you can't afford/justify the time to do a proper tax planning job, so the result is substandard. This leaves both the accountant and the client unsatisfied.

The minimum fees you should charge for tax planning are detailed in Chapter 7.

4. Number 3: Inadequate time spent on the tax planning process

Even if accountants are well-trained and use tax planning software, it will still take time to complete the tax planning process. Skipping any of the ten stages or not spending adequate time on a stage will result in a substandard result for the client. The tax planning report will be sub-optimal, and the client will pay more tax than they otherwise should.

5. Number 4: Failing to gather client information and data

Just as financial planners need to know their clients when preparing a financial plan, accountants need to know their clients when preparing a tax planning report. This involves gathering the client's information and data so the complete picture of the client's affairs can be analysed.

Accountants normally know their client's income and expenses, as this information is included in their compliance tax returns.

What is less well known is the client's assets and liabilities. Most accountants, even with long-term business clients, would have no idea of the client's net worth and their specific assets and liabilities.

6. Number 5: Inadequate tax strategies database

The tax strategies database is the intellectual knowledge and know-how that is the horsepower behind the whole tax planning process. A substandard or limited tax strategies database will not get the job done for the client and will inevitably produce poor performance. Too many accountants attempt to provide tax planning services with an arsenal or toolkit of only 10-20 tax strategies. The reality is that too many accountants are just relying on the negative gearing and super contributions tax strategies.

7. Number 6: Failing to provide the client with a written tax planning report that includes the implementation process and cost/benefits.

All important client advice should be provided in writing (irrespective of whether it was provided to the client verbally). This practice is recommended by both the ATO and professional bodies to protect both the client and the practice.

A tax planning report should be provided to the client at the advisory meeting (report presentation).

Providing the client with the written tax planning report achieves two objectives:

- Allows the client to review the report and consider the options in their own time. In an advisory meeting, a lot is discussed, and the client will not necessarily absorb and understand it all at the time (of course, you hope they will, but this is not always the case).
- Shows the client the tangible work put into the tax planning process. The problem with advice without a report is that

the client only thinks it's a five-minute consultation, so it's not worth anything. Producing the report addresses this weakness.

8. Number 7: Inadequate tax planning training

Most practice principals (80%) meet the Tax Practitioner Board requirements of forty hours of annual accounting and tax training. Unfortunately, this is normally exclusively related to their compliance-related services, with no training in value-added services such as tax planning or business advisory.

The second problem is that tax planning has historically been learned on the job or passed down by partners or managers. The lack of formal training courses has been a weakness and hindered the development of accountants' expertise in this area.

17.

Five advanced tax planning concepts

*'IN 1790, THE NATION WHICH HAD FOUGHT A REVOLUTION
AGAINST TAXATION WITHOUT REPRESENTATION DISCOVERED
THAT SOME OF ITS CITIZENS WEREN'T MUCH HAPPIER ABOUT
TAXATION WITH REPRESENTATION'*
– LYNDON B. JOHNSON.

1. Five advanced concepts

These five concepts provide extreme tax savings when implemented or make 'having fun' tax-deductible. What is not to like? The five advanced concepts are:

1. Making holidays deductible.
2. Utilise business goodwill to pay out your private mortgage.
3. Having fun in the workplace.
4. Change a hobby to a business.
5. All-inclusive holiday packages.

These are explained below.

2. Making holidays deductible

Business travel involves being away from home for at least one night for business purposes. This contrasts with other types of private travel such as 'for leisure purposes' or 'regularly commuting between one's home and workplace'. Business trips involve visiting customers or suppliers, meetings at other company locations, professional development, seminars, networking, etc. The expenses will need to be apportioned when the business travel is partly for business purposes and partly for private purposes (say a holiday). This is normally done on time by working out how many days in the trip related to business purposes, and how many private. Business travel days include:

- Travel days.
- Weekend days, which are sandwiched between two business days.
- Days where more than 50% of the day was spent on business activities.

Strategies to increase the client's travel deductions include:

- Hiring their spouse and children. If they are involved in the business and there is a legitimate business reason for them being on the business trip, their expenses will also be deductible.
- Attending seminars and conferences interstate and overseas. Hawaii, Las Vegas, London, and California are always popular!
- Taking their business car for family travel. A business trip that involves taking along family members in the car will still be a business trip, and the motor vehicle expenses will be 100% deductible.
- Taking business-related courses on cruise ships. Many professional organisations are now offering courses on cruise ships.
- When staying with friends on business trips, pay them an accommodation fee or gift them (both options will be deductible).
- Visiting potential clients and business associates to improve skills, get referrals, and experience new places.

3. Utilise business goodwill to pay out your private mortgage

This concept enables business owners to utilise the value of their business goodwill to pay out their private mortgage and convert a non-deductible mortgage into tax-deductible debt. The average Australian family pays over $25,000 annual interest on their $450,000 home mortgage. Making these interest payments tax-deductible will save them $10,000 tax year one, and $150,000 over the loan term. The actual process to achieve these tax savings depends on the taxpayer's personal circumstances and the entity type that operates the business. Expert advice is required to implement this to achieve tax savings without creating a capital gains tax liability during the business restructuring process. Also need to consider Part 4A implications.

For individuals operating the business as sole traders, implementing this involves selling the business at arms-length market values to a company or trust entity. The entity purchasing the business will get a bank loan to fund the purchase (with the interest being tax-deductible). The individual vendor will use the sale proceeds to pay their non-deductible private mortgage. Individuals operating a business in partnership have two options. Firstly, the partnership should get a loan to repay the partners' capital accounts (money originally advanced by a partner to fund the business). The interest on this loan will be tax-deductible. Secondly, the partnership sells the business at arms-length market values to a company or trust entity.

Unit trusts operating the business will get a bank loan to fund a unitholder buyback to reduce the paid-up capital to nil. The unit trust loan interest will be tax-deductible, and the unitholders will have the capital they originally invested in the unit trust returned tax-free.

Companies operating the business will get a bank loan to

fund a share buyback to reduce the paid-up capital to nil. The loan interest paid by the company will be tax-deductible, and the shareholders will have the capital they originally invested in the company returned tax-free. Alternatively, a shareholder in the company operating the business sells their shareholding at market values to their spouse or a related entity. The spouse purchases the shares utilising a new bank loan and claims the interest as a deduction (against expected future dividend income).

Individuals selling their business (whether as sole traders or partnerships), shares in companies, or units in unit trusts will be subject to capital gains tax when the sale proceeds exceed their cost bases. Small business entities with significant individuals can reduce these capital gains by 75% by applying the 12-month general discount and active asset discount. The last 25% of the gain can be eliminated by applying the replacement asset or retirement options.

4. Having fun in the workplace

Research shows that having fun in the workplace can significantly improve productivity and performance. As Richard Branson from Virgin says, "Happy employees make happy customers, which make happy shareholders. It all sounds so simple, but of course, it's not".

Having fun in the workplace:
- Increases morale and motivation,
- Develop a positive staff culture,
- Increases productivity and performance,
- Makes staff recruitment easier and less expensive,
- Improves teamwork,
- Enhances creativity,
- Resolves conflicts, and
- Improves employee loyalty.

The Australian Taxation Office has acknowledged that Australian workplaces have changed and that entertainment-related items increase employee productivity. An X-box, Foxtel, pinball machines, etc., can be purchased for office use during employees' work breaks. Each item of equipment that costs less than $20,000 will be tax-deductible upfront.

5. Change a hobby into a business

Changing a hobby into a business can make some private expenses tax-deductible. Expenses such as a motor vehicle, home office, travel, professional development, etc, may become deductible. Of course, the income generated will now be taxable, but the taxpayer will have an overall benefit if the expenses exceed the income. Whether the client is operating a business or hobby is a question of the facts. For example, two people could buy and sell rare coins on eBay, and for tax purposes, one could be a business and the other a hobby.

I WANT YOU
TO HAVE FUN
AT WORK.

Businesses have the following characteristics:

- The activity is planned, organised and carried on business-like. This may include keeping business records, operating a separate bank account, having licences or qualifications, having a registered business name, operating from business premises, etc.
- The size or scale of the activity is consistent with other businesses in the industry.
- The activities are repeated. For example, the taxpayer constantly buys and sells coins.
- The objective is to make a profit, even if it is unlikely to do so in the short term.
- The taxpayer decided to start a business and has registered an ABN or applied for a business name.

6. All-inclusive holiday package

Providing an all-inclusive holiday package to an employee organised through a travel agent that includes both flights and the hire or lease of holiday accommodation will be a single benefit whose taxable value is partly attributable to entertainment facility leasing expenses. As the benefit is partly attributable to entertainment facility leasing expenses, the whole package will be treated as an entertainment facility leasing expense.

This strategy involves using the 50-50 split method for entertainment facility leasing costs incurred by the employer. This means that 50% of the costs are non-deductible. The other 50% are deductible but subject to FBT. Under this option, the after-tax cost of $10,000 on an all-inclusive holiday package is $12,232. In contrast, an individual taxpayer in the 47% tax bracket would be $18,868.

Example of $10,000 incurred on holiday package:	
Flights and lease of holiday accommodation	$10,000
GST refunded (50% x $10,000 x 1/11)	(454)
Tax saving on ($4,546 expense x 25%))	(1,136)
FBT payable ($5,000 x 2.0802 x 49%)	5,096
Tax savings on FBT paid ($5,096 x 25%)	(1,274
Total after-tax cost	$12,232

Eifel Tower Paris – historical. It is one of the world's main tourist attractions.

18.

Fringe benefits you will love

1. Overview

Fringe benefits supplement an employee's 'money wage' or salary. When these benefits are provided to employees, they are tax-deductible to the employer, not assessable to the employee, and not subject to fringe benefits tax (FBT). This is a win for both the employer and the employee. Seven fringe benefits you will love are:

1. Salary packaging private motor vehicles
2. FBT exempt work-related items.
3. Taxi travel.
4. Salary packaging for FBT-exempt employees.
5. Remote area housing benefit.
6. FBT exemptions and reductions.
7. Employee meal expenses on business premises.

2. Salary packaging private motor vehicles

When a motor vehicle is used 100% for private purposes there is normally no tax deduction on the expenditure. With this strategy, employees can generate annual tax savings of $2,500 - $3,000 pa by salary packaging their private motor vehicle with their employer.

The tax savings result from the motor vehicle tax concessions available under the Fringe Benefits Tax Act and the GST savings on the motor vehicle expenses incurred. This will involve the employer owning or leasing the motor vehicle and providing the motor vehicle to the employee as a fringe benefit as part of the employee's overall salary package. The employer ensures the employee's overall salary package doesn't increase by reducing the cash salary paid to cover the motor vehicle and fringe benefits tax costs.

As such, it should also be used to salary package a spouse or children's motor vehicles if they are used for private purposes only.

3. FBT exempt work-related items

Providing the following work-related items to employees is tax-deductible and FBT-exempt:

- Portable electronic devices such as mobile phones, laptops, tablets, portable printers and GPS navigation receivers.
- Computer software.
- Protective clothing.
- Briefcases.
- Tools of trade.

Even when employees sacrifice their salary to pay for the items with their employer, they still benefit from saving the GST and having an upfront tax savings (instead of purchasing the item and depreciating it over several years in their tax return).

The FBT exemption is limited to items primarily for use in the employee's employment and one item per FBT year for items with a substantially identical function unless the item is a replacement item. An exception to this rule allows small businesses to provide employees with more than one work-related portable electronic device in an FBT year – even if the devices have substantially identical functions.

4. Taxi travel

Employer-provided Uber or taxi travel that is a single trip beginning or ending at the employee's place of work will be tax-deductible to the employer and an FBT-exempt benefit to the employee. This enables an employer to provide an employee with a single taxi trip to the office every day, and then another single trip home from the office every night (making the employee's home-to-work travel tax-deductible to the employer).

In addition, any benefit arising from taxi travel by an employee is also an exempt benefit if the travel is both:

- A result of sickness or injury to, the employee.
- The whole or a part of the journey directly between any of the following:
  o The employee's place of work.
  o The employee's place of residence.
  o Any other place that it is necessary, or appropriate, for the employee to go as a result of the sickness or injury.

One of the first taxis

5. Salary packaging for FBT-exempt employees

Certain public and non-profit hospitals, ambulance services, public benevolent institutions (PBIs), religious institutions, and health promotion charities (HPCs) are eligible for an FBT exemption. The benefits it provides its employees are exempt from FBT if the total grossed-up value of certain benefits for each employee during the FBT year is equal to, or less than, the capping threshold. If the total grossed-up value of fringe benefits provided to an employee is more than the capping threshold, the employer will need to pay FBT on the excess.

The FBT capping thresholds are:
- PBIs - (other than hospitals) - $31,177 per employee.
- HPCs - $31,177 per employee.
- Public and not-for-profit hospitals - $17,667 per employee.
- Public ambulance services - $17,667 per employee.
- Religious institutions for benefits provided to religious practitioners – no cap applies.

Car parking benefits are excluded from the FBT capping thresholds. From April 1, 2016, only the first $5,000 of meal entertainment and entertainment facility leasing expenses are excluded from the FBT capping thresholds.

6. Remote area housing benefits

A remote area housing benefit is exempt under section 58ZC of the Fringe Benefits Tax Assessment Act 1986. If a housing benefit is deemed a remote area housing benefit, the employer can claim a tax deduction for the employee's housing costs, and no FBT is payable. This converts an employee's private housing costs into a tax-deductible expense. A housing benefit qualifies as a remote area housing benefit where:

- For the whole of the tenancy period, the unit of accommodation is in a remote area (that is, it is not located in or adjacent to an eligible urban area).
- For the whole tenancy period, the accommodation is occupied by a person who is a current employee, and the usual place of employment of the employee is in a remote area.
- The benefit was not provided to the employee under either a non-arm's length arrangement or an arrangement entered into by any of the parties for the purpose, or partial purpose, of obtaining the concession.
- It would be concluded that it must be necessary for the employer to provide accommodation for employees or to arrange to provide such accommodation because:
  o The nature of their business is such that employees are liable to move frequently from one residential location to another.
  o There is insufficient suitable residential accommodation otherwise available at or near the place or places where the employees are employed or
  o It is customary for employers in that industry to provide free or subsidised accommodation for employees.

Accommodation is classified as being near or adjacent to an eligible urban area and, therefore not remote where it is situated either:

- Less than 40 kilometres from an eligible urban area with a census population of 14,000 to less than 130,000.
- Less than 100 kilometres from an eligible urban area with a census population of 130,000 or more.

7. FBT exemptions and reductions

Benefits the FBT exemptions and reductions apply to include:

- Long service awards: The benefit provided to an employee is limited to $1,000 plus $100 for each year of service that exceeds 15 years.
- Motor vehicles.
- Safety awards – limited to $200 per employee per FBT year.
- In-house benefits reduction – limited to $1,000 per employee per year.
- Superannuation contributions.
- Work-related items, protective clothing, tools, mobile phones, and laptops.
- Taxi travel (to or from work).
- Remote area housing.
- Work-related medical and health counselling and care.
- Migrant language training.
- Fly-in-fly-out arrangements (transport from an employee's home base to a remote area work site.
- Overseas employment and trips home.
- School fees for employees posted overseas.
- Employee relocation costs (travel costs, furniture transport, plus home sale and purchase costs).
- Living away from home allowances (partly exempt).
- Employee relocation costs (including relocation travel costs, furniture removal, temporary accommodation, meal travel costs, and home sale and purchase costs).

8. Employee meal expenses on business premises

Employee meal costs, like lunch during a normal workday, are normally private non-deductible expenses. But an employer can provide the following meals to employees, claim a tax deduction for the expenses, and pay no fringe benefits tax:

- Tea, coffee and cakes provided on business premises for employees and customers.
- Sandwiches, muffins, fruit, pastries, etc. consumed during a work meeting or training session on business premises.
- A light meal and drink consumed on business premises while working. This includes pizza, takeaway food, drinks, etc.

By providing employees with free meals during a workday employers benefit from increased employee satisfaction, easier employee recruitment (as employees are getting a free benefit not provided by most employers), and increased employee productivity (as employees are more likely to work longer hours if they don't need to leave the business premises for meals).

Business owners operating their business through a trust or company structure are also employees of the business. As such the business can also claim a tax deduction for their meal expenses when it meets the criteria detailed above.

19.

Tax saving entities

1. 10 tax saving entities

The 10 tax-saving entities discussed below all do as their name suggests – that is, save tax. Of course, tax-saving entities should be chosen based on the best matching of the client's unique circumstances. The 'best' 10 tax saving entities are:

1. Companies.
2. Holding company.
3. Unit trusts.
4. Husband and wife partnerships.
5. PSI entity.
6. Discretionary trust.
7. Self-managed super fund.
8. Testamentary trust.
9. Partnership of discretionary trusts.
10. Special disability trust.

2. Companies

The advantages of operating a business through a company include:

- 30% tax rate (standard company tax rate).
- 25% tax rate for companies with a turnover less than $50,000,000 pa.
- Limited liability – this ensures the shareholder's liability is limited to the capital invested in the company.
- The ability for investors to pool their investment funds together.

The World's Oldest Businesses

Japan contains the oldest business in a variety of trades and industries

Type of Business	Name	Country	Year Founded
Oldest Hotel	Nishiyama Onsen Keiunkan	Japan	705
Oldest Machinery Company	TECH Kaihatsu	Japan	760
Oldest Restaurant	Stiftskeller St. Peter	Austria	803
Oldest Winery	Staffelter Hof	Germany	862
Oldest Religious Goods Company	Tanaka-Iga	Japan	885
Oldest Pub	Sean's Bar	Ireland	900
Oldest Confectionary	Ichimonjiya Wasuke	Japan	1000
Oldest Brewery	Weihenstephan	Germany	1040
Oldest Tea Company	Tsuen Tea	Japan	1160
Oldest Metalwork Company	Ito Tekko	Japan	1189
Oldest Sake Company	Sudo Honke	Japan	1141
Oldest Pharmacy	Sankogan	Japan	1319

The main disadvantage of operating through a company is that it doesn't receive the 50% general capital gain discount like individuals. In addition, the extra compliance and regulatory costs and directors' legal obligations and duties need to be considered. Ideally, the company shareholder should be a family trust (not the individual directors). This provides flexibility and enables future distributions of dividends and capital gains to be distributed to lower-taxed beneficiaries (as well as providing asset protection benefits).

3. Holding Companies

A holding company is a parent corporation that owns enough voting shares in another company to control its policies and management. It exists solely to control one or several other companies and to own property such as real estate, patents, trademarks, shares, and other assets. If a business is 100% owned by a holding company, it is called a wholly-owned subsidiary.

The benefits of forming a holding company include:

- The holding company is protected from losses if a subsidiary company fails and goes into liquidation. The subsidiary company's creditors have no claim against the holding company's assets.

- Different company assets can be transferred to subsidiary companies. For example, one subsidiary may own the brand name and trademarks, another real estate, another equipment, and another to operate the trading business.
- Subsidiary companies may be located and operate in a country other than the parent company's. The subsidiary most likely has its own senior management structure, products, and clients.
- The ability to reduce subsidiary costs by having the holding company provide certain centralised services such as finance, administration, marketing, financial systems, etc.
- Holding companies can raise equity capital and loan funds much more easily and cheaply than an individual subsidiary company (as it provides investors and lenders lower risk than a subsidiary company).

The tax advantages of holding companies include:
- Can apply the tax consolidation regime to wholly-owned subsidiaries so that the losses of one group company are available to the whole consolidated entity. In addition, intergroup transactions are eliminated for tax purposes.
- Holding companies can be based in low-tax countries. Pepsi, for example, is based in Denmark, and holding companies pay no tax there.
- Franked dividends paid to the holding company are effectively tax-free.
- The holding company can charge the subsidiary companies for services provided and shift profits (subject to arms-length transfer prices being charged).

4. Unit Trust

Unit trusts are attractive when non-related parties want to join together to operate a business or make investments. Unit trust structures have the following advantages:

- Ability to access tax-free distributions. This is especially important for property trusts where the cash flows generated are normally higher than the taxable income (due to the non-cash building and depreciation write-offs).
- The unitholders receive the general 50% CGT discount on any capital gains made by the unit trust on investments for more than twelve months. In contrast, companies do not receive the general 50% CGT discount.
- Each party's investment interest is fixed through their ownership of units in the unit trust (similar to company shares).
- Ability to pool resources with other investors.
- The unit trust profits are distributed to the unitholders in proportion to their percentage unitholding in the trust. Each unitholder is taxed on their trust distribution at their marginal tax rates.
- Easy to introduce new investors into the unit trust or exit other unitholders.
- Limited liability if the trustee is a company.

A disadvantage of unit trusts and trusts, in general, is that they cannot distribute losses to the unitholders. Any losses incurred by the unit trust must be carried forward to be offset against future income. Where non-related parties use unit trust structures, they should have a written unitholder agreement to protect their interests and deal with any inevitable disputes. Consider whether the unit trust unitholder should be a family trust (not individuals). This provides flexibility and enables future distributions of dividends and capital gains to be distributed to lower-taxed beneficiaries (as well as providing asset protection benefits).

5. Husband and Wife Partnerships

The ATO look at the following factors in deciding whether persons are carrying on a business as partners for tax purposes:

- The mutual assent and intention of the parties,
- Joint ownership of business assets,
- The extent to which the parties are involved in the conduct of the business,
- Business records,
- Joint business bank account, and
- Trading in joint names and public recognition of the partnership.

In a typical husband and wife partnership, one partner is qualified (for example, an electrician) and produces the partnership income, and the other partner may be involved in the administration of the partnership. Profits from the partnership are normally split 50/50 between the partners. The ATO reviewed this structure in 2005 in their 'Refocus of the income-splitting test case programme' and accepted it as legitimate because both partners are exposed to the liability for the partnership debts, so both should share the rewards. Tradespeople using husband and wife partnerships can generate substantial tax savings where one spouse has low or no other income. Unfortunately, this only applies to tradespeople partnerships (so doesn't apply to husband and wife computer services, engineering consulting, etc.).

6. PSI Entity

Personal services income (PSI) is mainly from an individual's skills or efforts. Typically, more than 50% of the income from a contract is for an individual's skills, knowledge, expertise, or efforts. It's income that has the characteristics of employment income. PSI income generated through an entity (company or trust) will still be the PSI income of the individual generating the income, and they will be taxed on that income in their personal tax return.

But irrespective of that, receiving PSI income through an entity still has the following advantages:

- Reduced risk, as contracts are with an entity instead of directly with the individual; therefore, the individual's personal assets are protected.
- Normal business expenses will be deductible to the entity. This includes advertising, rent, accountant's fees, telephone, wages to non-related parties, travel, and training.
- Superannuation is deductible for the principal up to the deductible contributions limit.
- Can provide the individual with concessionally taxed fringe benefits such as a living away from home allowance or relocation-based benefits. This can make private accommodation and meal expenses deductible.
- Deduction for exempt benefits such as laptop computers, tools of trade and phones provided to the individual.
- You can receive tax deductions for two motor vehicles, but only one can be used for private purposes (which can actually be 100% private).

7. Discretionary Trust

Discretionary trusts are attractive business structures as they can provide the following benefits:

- Flexibility with income distributions (income can be allocated in different amounts and to different beneficiaries yearly).
- Asset protection.

- Access to the 50% general CGT discount.

If a discretionary trust has a large taxable income, it may not want to distribute all the taxable income to individual taxpayers. This is because the individuals may end up paying tax on this income at up to 47%. To avoid this situation, the trust may include a 'bucket company' as a beneficiary of the trust and distribute some income to it.

The tax advantage of this strategy is that the company will only be taxed at 25% on this income. An additional benefit of this strategy is risk management, as investments are accumulated in an entity separate from the business structure (i.e. trust). A low-risk spouse or associate should own the shares in the investment 'bucket company'. With this strategy, the income distributed to the company for tax purposes will generally need to be physically paid to the company before the date the company lodges its tax return with the ATO.

Once the company receives the trust distribution, it can pay 25% of the tax liability and invest 75% into term deposits, shares, or property. Problems arise with this strategy when the trust doesn't physically have the cash available to pay the company beneficiary. This causes Division 7A loan issues, which can result in more taxes payable.

8. Self-Managed Super Fund

This strategy involves a taxpayer selling listed securities (whether shares or managed funds) and commercial properties into their super fund. The title of the investments is then in the super fund name and the super fund accounts for any income generated by the investments. The sale of the investments needs to be done at market prices. It may involve a tax liability for the taxpayer (depending on the taxpayer's original cost price of the investments, the market prices on the date of transfer, and whether any small business CGT concessions apply). In addition, if a commercial property is sold to a super fund, stamp duty costs will need to be considered. Stamp duty costs vary greatly depending on the State Government involved, from nil to concessional stamp duty to full stamp duty rates.

The benefits of this strategy include:

- The individual can receive a tax deduction for super contributions into the super fund that are satisfied by transferring the investments (subject to the concessional superannuation contributions caps).
- The tax payable on the investment income generated by the super fund investments is taxed at a maximum rate of 15% and can be as low as 0%.
- Investments in a super fund are protected and quarantined if an individual goes bankrupt.
- Depending on the super fund's taxable income, the ATO may refund part or all of the imputation credits on the super fund's investments.

9. Testamentary Trust

A testamentary trust (sometimes referred to as a will trust or trust under the will) is a trust that arises upon the death of the trustor and is specified in his or her will. The three parties involved in a testamentary trust are:

- The trustor —The person who specifies that the trust is created and contributes property to it, usually through his or her will.
- The trustee – This person administers the will as per the instructions in the will.
- The beneficiary(s) – This is the person or people who will benefit from the assets the trust holds.

Effectively, on the date of death, certain deceased assets pass across to a testamentary trust where they are held on behalf of beneficiaries. Beneficiaries may have either a fixed or discretionary entitlement to income and assets from the trust. The advantages of a testamentary trust include:

- Minor beneficiaries (i.e. under 18 years of age) are not taxed at penalty tax rates on any income distributed to them from the trust. Instead, they are taxed at the adult marginal tax rates, so they benefit from the $18,200 tax-free threshold.
- No CGT when assets pass to beneficiaries.
- Income splitting and income streaming opportunities.
- Protects assets from creditors and vulnerable beneficiaries.

The implementation process involves a solicitor incorporating a testamentary trust into the will of the trustor. This is an optimum structure that allows grandparents to transfer assets on their death to their grandchildren in a tax-effective manner (even if the children are under 18).

10. Partnership of Discretionary Trusts

A partnership of discretionary trusts is a partnership where each partner is a discretionary trust. This is a good structure for unrelated parties wanting to operate a business or invest together because:

- Provides each partner with a fixed interest—say 50% each.
- Allows access to the CGT small business concessions.
- Asset protection (when set up with a company as the trustee of each discretionary trust).
- Flexibility in splitting profits amongst family members.
- Simple to establish and relatively easy to dissolve.
- Partners are not employees so superannuation contributions and workers' compensation insurance are not payable.

- Shared management, combined skills, experience and knowledge can produce a better product or service.

11. Special Disability Trust

A Special Disability Trust is a trust established primarily for succession planning by parents and immediate family members for the current and future care and accommodation needs of a person with a severe disability or medical condition. The general approach is that the trust can pay for any care, accommodation, medical costs and other needs of the beneficiary during their lifetime.

A Special Disability Trust is not the same as a normal trust. It needs to be established by a solicitor and strictly drafted to include the compulsory clauses of the Model Trust Deed as set down in the legislation. In addition, before a Special Disability Trust is established, the prospective trust beneficiary must be assessed as severely disabled under the legislation for this type of trust. Further details are available at www.dss.gov.au.

Once a disability trust is established, family members can transfer property, shares, and cash to the trust. The income from the trust will then be used to provide for the disabled person's future care and accommodation. The trustee of the disability trust will be taxed annually on the trust income at individual marginal tax rates. A capital gains tax exemption (CGT) applies to CGT assets transferred into the disability trust for no consideration. This allows family members to provide for the disabled person by transferring CGT assets without personally incurring capital gains tax liabilities. In addition, if the Special Disability Trust acquires a residence for the trust beneficiary to live in, the capital gains tax main residence exemption will apply to it. The capital gains tax exemption also applies to the recipient of the beneficiary's main residence if the main residence is disposed of within two years of the beneficiary's death.

12. Final Word

The world is constantly changing, as are the taxpayer's circumstances. What was the ideal and most tax-effective entity for the taxpayer ten years ago, five years ago, or even last year may not be so today. At least annually, all tax-saving entities should be reviewed to see whether they are achieving the result they were set up to achieve or whether another entity type would better suit the taxpayer's current circumstances. If the review determines that the entity is no longer needed, it should be wound up to save ongoing compliance costs.

20.
Tax-saving investments

1. Holiday homes

Taxpayers who own holiday homes for generating rental income (even part-time) will be entitled to claim certain rental property expenses as a tax deduction. The deductible rental expenses for a holiday home are the same as for a normal rental property, i.e. interest, depreciation, building write-off, rates, taxes, repairs, and management fees. With income-generating holiday homes, as the property is used for both income-producing and private purposes (e.g., own private use), the rental expenses must be apportioned between the deductible and non-deductible percentages.

The expenses are normally apportioned on time to calculate the deductible percentage. That is the percentage of the year the property is rented or available for rent. So, for example, if the property were rented or available for rent 40% of the time, then 40% of the rental property expenses would be deductible. The ATO deems a property available for rent if it is listed for rent with a real estate management agent. If there is uncertainty about the correctness of claiming rental property losses on a holiday house, the ATO's policy is to limit the deductions to the amount of rental income received.

Three key investment principles with purchasing a holiday home:

- Purchasing a holiday house in an area where the client wishes to retire in locks in their future retirement property at today's prices.

- Freestanding holiday houses have more potential capital gains than apartments due to the flexibility to improve the properties or subdivide in the future.
- The ideal location is where the holiday house can be rented for returns similar to traditional rental properties.

The holiday home must be listed for rent with a real estate management agent. Diary records should be kept recording when the property is available for rent, rented, and used for private purposes. The property cannot be used for 100% private purposes during peak rental periods such as Christmas, Easter, school holidays, and public holidays to maximise tax savings.

2. Agribusiness schemes

The ATO treats investors in agribusiness schemes as primary producers carrying on a business in agriculture, forestry or horticulture for the purpose of generating income. This means the ATO applies the same tax treatment to agribusiness managed investment scheme investors as they do to farmers. These schemes are typically very tax efficient as the investments are structured so the majority of the investment is tax-deductible (whether in year one or over several years). For an investor in the top tax bracket of 47%, a $10,000 investment could produce a $4,700 tax refund.

Some of the risks involved in investing in agribusiness schemes include — the scheme may run out of money and fold, the requirement to make additional annual payments for management fees, the returns are hard to predict as the weather, demand, worldwide prices, crop yields, and costs are subject to wide annual fluctuations, and the investment is poorly diversified. Review the ATO Product Ruling to determine what components of the total investment cost are deductible upfront, what are deductible over several years, and what are non-deductible capital.

3. Negative gearing

Negative gearing is where borrowed funds are used to invest in either property or shares, and the income generated (at least in the short term) is less than the tax-deductible expenses. This creates a taxable loss from the investment, which may be offset against the taxpayer's other income (normally salary and wage income). This results in the salary and wage earner receiving a tax refund of part of the PAYG withholding tax they have had deducted from their wages over the year. This is a profitable strategy if the investment grows in value (capital appreciation) each year, by an amount greater than the taxable loss less the tax refund received, less the depreciation claimed. The strategy works best when the purchased investments produce stable income and yearly capital appreciation.

The risks involved when borrowing to invest include:

- Income risk - The taxpayer loses their job or income source and cannot fund the taxable loss.
- Capital risk - The investments purchased fall in value or stay constant.
- Investment income risk —The investment doesn't produce the expected investment income, e.g., the rental property becomes unrented, or the dividend-paying shares stop paying dividends.
- Interest rate risk – Interest rates on the loan could rise.

4. Art

Small businesses buying art prior to 30th June 2025 with a purchase cost of less than $20,000 (excluding GST) are entitled to a full tax deduction. The art can be enjoyed at the small business's office, warehouse, farm, or home office. There are no restrictions on the type of art or the number of pieces purchased.

After 1st July 2025, the upfront deduction is only available for individual art pieces costing less than $1,000 each. Where art costs more than $1,000 the asset will instead go into the general pool and be depreciated at 15% in the first year of purchase, and 30% per year after that. Irrespective of the art's purchase price, all GST registered businesses are entitled to claim an input tax credit back on the purchase price (where the artist or gallery charged GST on the sale). This means the ATO is effectively funding 1/11 of the upfront cost.

Art in the workplace has been proven to reduce stress, increase productivity, improve communication and stimulate creative thinking. In a recent survey, 82% of employees said art was important in their work environment, and 73% said they would change employers if the art were removed. In addition, art is a great investment and has produced long-term annual capital gains of 4-5% over the last 465 years.

5. Farm management deposits

The Farm Management Deposits (FMD) scheme allows eligible primary producers to move income from a year in which they don't need it, to a later year when they need the income. This is achieved by allowing the primary producer a deduction in the financial year in which they make an eligible deposit to the FMD account (which is a special bank account with an institution that accepts farm management deposits). When the primary producer withdraws funds from the FMD account, that income is assessable and is included in their tax return as income.

Farm management deposits are deductible if all of the following are satisfied:

- The taxable non-primary production income is less than $100,000.
- The taxpayer is carrying on a primary production business at the time of making the deposit.
- The individual deposits are not less than $1,000 and total deposits not more than $800,000.
- Individual deposits do not exceed the amount of the taxpayer's taxable primary production income.
- The deposits are held for at least 12 months or qualify for one of the early repayment exemptions.
- If the taxpayer stopped carrying on a primary production business during the year, they recommenced carrying on the business within 120 days.
- The taxpayer is not deceased.

6. Concessional superannuation contributions

This strategy involves a taxpayer making concessional superannuation contributions. The super contributions are either contributed to a public offer fund or a self-managed super fund and invested into a mixture of cash, shares, bonds, commodities and property.

Superannuation funds can pay three different rates of tax:
- 0% - When in 100% pension phase.
- 10% - On any capital gains when the asset was owned for more than 12 months.
- 15% - Other taxable income.

7. Early-stage investors

The tax incentives provide concessional tax treatment for investors including:
- A 20% non-refundable tax offset on investments, capped at $200,000 per investor per year.
- A capital gains tax exemption provided investments are held for at least one year and less than ten years.
- Requiring that the investor and the innovation company are non-affiliates and the investor owns less than 30% of the company.
- Limiting the investment amount for non-sophisticated investors to qualify for the tax offset to $50,000 or less per income year.

The tax incentives will only be available for investments in companies that:
- Satisfy a 100-point innovation test or are companies that are genuinely focused on developing for commercialisation new or improved products, processes services or methods and can demonstrate that certain requirements in relation to the commercialisation of the innovation are satisfied (for example, that the business related to the innovation has a high growth potential, and the company has the potential to scale its activities to take advantage of the growth potential).
- Were incorporated during the last three income years.

- Are not listed on any stock exchange.
- Have expenditure of less than $1 million in the previous income year.
- Have an income of less than $200,000 in the previous income year.

The early-stage tax incentives apply to all types of taxpayers including individuals, companies, partners, trusts, and super funds.

8. Exploration Development Incentive

The Exploration Development Incentive (EDI) encourages shareholder investment in small exploration companies under-taking greenfield mineral exploration in Australia. It provides an economic incentive to invest in the Australian mining sector. The EDI enables eligible exploration companies to create exploration credits by giving up a portion of their tax losses from greenfield minerals expenditure and distributing these exploration credits to equity shareholders. Australian resident shareholders who are issued with an exploration credit will be entitled to a refundable tax offset or additional franking credits. The exploration company's carried forward losses are reduced proportionately to reflect the amount of exploration credits created.

Eligible exploration companies can create exploration credits if they are a disclosing entity that:
- Has incurred greenfields (exploration and prospecting) minerals expenditure in the previous year.
- Have not carried on any mining operations for the ex-traction of minerals in the previous two years.
- Have notified the ATO of their estimated greenfields minerals expenditure and estimated tax loss for the previous income year by 30th September of the financial

year in which it is intended to create exploration credits.

Shareholders may claim the tax offset in the income year in which they receive the exploration credits. For example, green-field minerals expenditure incurred by a company in the 2024/25 income year requires the company to notify the ATO of participation in the incentive by 30th September 2025. The exploration credit is then created and issued to the shareholders during 2024/25 income year (and the tax offset claimed by the shareholder in their 2024/25 tax return).

9. Antique, veteran or vintage car

First Holden motor vehicle produced in Australia

The purchase of an antique, veteran or vintage car for use in a business will provide the normal depreciation and operating deductions. This will be subject to the luxury car limit and logbook obligation for business use. Motor vehicles, including antique, veteran and vintage cars, are exempt from capital gains. This is a win for collectable car owners as collectable cars have shown to appreciate in value over time. This is in direct contrast with the average motor vehicle which eventually ends up pretty worthless.

10. Purchase a farm or winery

This strategy involves using a SMSF to purchase a farm or winery and then leasing it back to the taxpayer (or associated entity) to operate the farm or winery. This strategy has the following attractions:

- Ability to combine the superannuation fund balances of up to 6 family members to purchase the farm.
- The superannuation fund can finance the purchase of the farm.
- The arms-length lease rental income payable to the SMSF is only taxed at 15% (or nil if in pension phase).
- The taxpayer (or associated entity) operates the farming business and can access all the primary production-related tax concessions including an immediate write-off for fencing and water facilities.
- The taxpayer operating the farming business receives a tax deduction for the farm rental payments made.

11. Investment reality check

Tax-saving investments only make economic sense if the investment grows in value (capital appreciation) each year, by an amount that is greater than the taxable loss less the tax refund received.

21.

Tax-free retirement

1. Seven strategies to maximise your return

Seven strategies to maximise the return in the SMSF are:

1. Start a pension in a SMSF.
2. SMSFs and shares.
3. Transfer personal investments in super.
4. Using a SMSF to undertake property development.
5. Transferring business premises into a SMSF.
6. Self-managed super fund borrowings.
7. SMSFs investing in non-controlled entities.

These are described below:

2. Start a pension in a SMSF

This strategy involves starting a pension in the SMSF so that the income the complying SMSF earns from assets held to provide for super income stream benefits is exempt from income tax. This is referred to as exempt current pension income (ECPI). This tax concession means that capital gains accrued on superannuation assets during the fund's accumulation phase will be exempt if the assets are sold after the fund has moved to the pension phase.

A SMSF can only start paying a member a pension if it has met one of the eleven conditions of release. The two most common conditions of release applied are:

- Reaching age 65 – no restrictions apply.
- Ceases an employment arrangement after reaching 60 years of age.

In 2024/25, a member's pension fund balance is limited to $1.9 million (which is indexed over time). The earnings generated by investing the $1.9 million are exempt from tax. Members with additional super fund balances must move the excess into the accumulation phase (where the earnings are subject to a 15% tax rate).

3. SMSFs and shares

A major tax advantage of owning shares in a SMSF is that any fully franked dividends received will have attached franking credits (which allow the SMSF a credit for the 30% tax paid by the company). As the super fund's tax rate is either 0% or 15% there will be excess franking credits available to reduce the tax payable on other super fund income or be refunded.

4. Transfer personal investments into super

This strategy involves a taxpayer selling listed securities (whether shares or managed funds) and commercial properties into their super fund. The title of the investments is then in the super fund name and the super fund accounts for any income generated by the investments. The sale of the investments needs to be done at market prices and may involve a tax liability for the taxpayer (depending on the taxpayer's original cost price of the investments, the market prices on the date of transfer, and whether any small business CGT concessions apply). In addition, if a commercial property is sold to a super fund then stamp duty costs will need to be considered. Stamp duty costs vary greatly depending on the State Government involved and vary from nil, to concessional stamp duty, to full stamp duty rates.

5. Using a SMSF to undertake a property development

Undertaking a property development in a SMSF can result in zero tax payable if the fund is in the pension phase. Assuming the trust deed allows it a SMSF can undertake a property development as there is nothing specifically in the investment rules or superannuation law that prevents it. The ATO has confirmed this in their online publication 'Thinking about self-managed super', that SMSF trustees can undertake property development.

Extra care must be undertaken to ensure that the super fund complies with the SIS Act including:

- The arm's length rules under S.109.
- The sole purpose test under S.62.
- Complies with the investment strategy of the fund.
- That any borrowings are for a single acquirable asset and comply with S.67A.
- Assets are not acquired from related parties and breach S.66.

6. Transferring business premises into a SMSF

This strategy involves a business owner transferring their business premises into their self-managed super fund (SMSF). This has the following advantages:

- Rent paid to the SMSF is taxed at between 0-15% in the SMSF.
- The business receives a tax deduction for any rent paid to the SMSF.
- When the SMSF sells the premises any capital gain will be taxed at between 0- 10%.
- Asset protection – SMSF assets are protected in the event the business or owner has financial difficulties.

7. Self-managed super fund borrowings

The general rule is that self-managed super funds are prohibited from having any borrowings. As an exception to that rule, since 2007 super funds can finance investments with limited recourse borrowing arrangements if they comply with section 67A of the SISA. Limited recourse borrowing arrangements must comply with the following:

- The borrowing is only permitted over a single asset or a collection of identical assets that have the same market value, e.g. one property or one parcel of BHP shares.
- The recourse of the lender against the super fund on default is limited to the single asset that was financed under the limited recourse loan. This means that all the super fund's other assets are protected.
- Super funds cannot borrow to improve an asset (for example real property).

The advantage of borrowing in a super fund is that the capital gains can be magnified and also the super fund benefits from negative gearing (so tax can be saved). All borrowing entails risks so the super fund needs to ensure that it has sufficient income (from investment earnings or employer/member contributions) to meet the loan repayments and expenses on the borrowings. The ultimate aim with self-managed super funds is to build a portfolio of investment-earning assets (a mix of term deposits, shares and property), so that on retirement when the fund is put into the pension phase, 100% of the fund earnings will be tax-free.

8. SMSFs investing in non-controlled entities

This strategy involves a SMSF investing in non-controlled unit trusts or companies. As the entities are non-controlled entities they can operate businesses, be geared, and invest without breaching the SIS legislation. This structure allows multiple unrelated SMSFs to invest in these entities and have the trust distributions, dividends, and capital gains taxed at the SMSF concessional tax rates (i.e. between 0 – 15%).

The key requirement is that the SMSF must not control the entity. This requires ownership of less than 50% of the entity, and ideally, less than 33%. In addition, the trustees/directors of the fund must ensure that the other investors in the non-controlled entities are not members of the fund, an employer-sponsor of the fund, or an associate of either the member or employer-sponsor.

9. Final word

A couple can jointly have $3.8 million invested in a SMSF which is in the pension phase and pay no tax. If the $3.8 million was invested in a diversified portfolio of shares paying an average 5% dividend yield the annual tax-free income would be $190,000. In addition, the $81,428 imputation credits would be refundable, increasing the total annual tax-free income to $271,428. In addition, historically share portfolios have produced capital gains greater than inflation (so the real value of the income and investments grow over time).

www.ingramcontent.com/pod-product-compliance
Lightning Source LLC
Chambersburg PA
CBHW042117190326
41519CB00030B/7533